Photo Guide

ROME

The Swiss Guard – the Pope's bodyguard – has a history stretching back over 500 years. Here, newly-sworn-in guards take part in a mass in St Peter's.

Photo Guide

ROME

The Piazza della Rotonda, named after the Pantheon, is one of the most beautiful and atmospheric squares in the city: a setting for romance, and a meeting point for young and old, by day and night.

ABOUT THIS BOOK

"While stands the Coliseum, Rome shall stand;
When falls the Coliseum, Rome shall fall;
And when Rome falls – the World."

Lord Byron, *Childe Harold's Pilgrimage*

Some 3,000 years ago, Rome's first settlers occupied a bend in the Tiber, the heart of today's Rome. Traces of them still remain, which is why Rome attracts anyone interested in history and culture. Walking through the Eternal City, the presence of its mythical founder, King Romulus, is felt as strongly as that of the great emperors of ancient Rome, when the city governed much of the world, or the popes who ruled the city in Renaissance and baroque times. In Rome, as in no other city, you can see the roots of Western civilization.

But Rome is not a museum. In the shadow of millennia-old monuments, life is lived in an infectious, truly *vitale* way. The city's restaurants, bars, markets, streets, and squares are filled with the bustle of business. The atmosphere is lively and stimulating, the Roman temperament echoing the hectic pace of Latin life, but life in Rome does not always have to be lived in the fast lane. As Goethe said: "Here the current takes you away as soon as you step into the boat".

One of the chief destinations on the Grand Tour for wealthy Europeans in the 18th and 19th centuries, Rome now attracts millions of visitors every year – as Robert Browning said: "Every one soon or late comes round by Rome".

Rome is part of a unique new series. *Photo Guides* combine two types of book in one: a beautifully photographed "coffee-table" book and an informative travel guide; each book is therefore a handy companion for its respective city. There are over 400 stunning photos and useful maps, with detailed information about the highlights of the city, festivals, and the real life of its citizens, district by district. There are features about special cultural events, history, and gastronomy, an informative timeline to guide you through the different ages of the city, guided walks with expert tips on shopping, eating, and accommodation, descriptions of the top museums, and, of course, all the important addresses. Each *Photo Guide* concludes with a large map of the city, street index, and website addresses.

Note: The international telephone code for Italy is 00 39. This is followed by the area code, e.g. 06 for Rome. The full area code must always be used, whether calling from abroad (e.g. 00 39 06 1234 5678) or within Italy (06 1234 5678). Only omit 0 from the area code when using a mobile (cell) phone.

The city, the river, and the dome of St Peter's. At night the shadows of the past seem to rise up from the waters of the Tiber and hover peacefully over the roofs of the Eternal City.

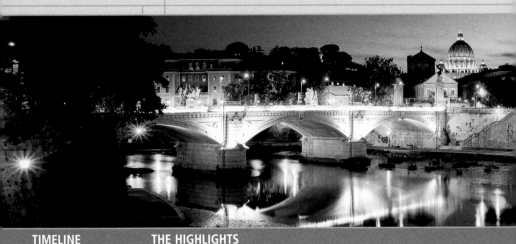

TIMELINE

THE HIGHLIGHTS

CONTENTS

"My Rome? – Not even Nero allowed himself to speak of 'his' Rome", said the journalist Franca Magnani, a Roman by birth. A city could never belong to just one person. So on the one hand, Rome belongs to no one – not the Romans, because they have to share their treasures with awestruck tourists, and not the tourists, because they are only here as guests. On the other hand, Rome belongs to all who enter this city and understand it, as did Federico Fellini when he said, "Rome is a carousel of memories, real events, and dreams".

CITY EXPLORER

CITY ATLAS

Napoleon once remarked that the history of Rome was also the history of Western civilization. If you follow the development of the city from its beginnings in about 1000 BC to the present day – from a primitive settlement of huts to a modern city – you will have an overview of the development of European culture, but you will see that it did not always follow an upward curve. On its path from its origins as the glorious heart of a global empire, through the seat of Christianity, to the capital of Italy: Rome, the Eternal City, had to overcome many setbacks before returning to its former brilliance.

The poets Virgil and Livy were convinced that the Romans had been *princeps terrarum populi*, the first people on earth. Many painters, especially during the Renaissance, took their themes from the myths of the city's foundation. From left: *Aeneas' Flight from Troy* (Federico Barocci, 1598); *The Apotheosis of Aeneas* (Pietro da Cortona, 1651); *Mars and Rhea Silvia* (Peter Paul Rubens, *circa* 1616).

The mythical past

According to legend, after a long war Troy was conquered by the Greeks, using the Trojan Horse.

...

Under the leadership of the hero Aeneas, fleeing Trojans land in Italy.

...

Aeneas' son Ascanius founds the city of Alba Longa, to the south of contemporary Rome.

...

Numitor, the king of Alba Longa, is overthrown by his brother Amulius.

...

Rhea Silvia, Numitor's daughter, gives birth to the twins Romulus and Remus, whose father is said to be Mars, the Roman god of war.

...

The usurper Amulius abandons the twin boys on the banks of the Tiber.

...

A she-wolf saves the children from death by protecting and suckling them.

...

Amulius is overthrown by Romulus and Remus, as the grandsons of the rightful ruler.

...

Romulus kills his brother in a fight; he founds the city named after himself on the Palatine Hill.

Around 1000 BC

Evidence of an Iron Age hut settlement has been found on the Palatine Hill.

Gods and heroes

In the 3rd century BC, when Rome proudly called itself *caput mundi*, the capital of the world, the legend of the foundation of this powerful city was well known. In his epic poem the *Aeneid*, Virgil (70–19 BC) told the story of Aeneas – the son of a king and the goddess Aphrodite – who defended the city of Troy for a long time against the attacking Greeks. According to the poet, when the Greek hero Odysseus finally managed to break the resistance of the defenders, Aeneas and his son fled with a small trusty band of followers. After a long voyage, the group was driven onto the coast of Italy, where Aeneas married Lavinia, the daughter of a local leader. Their son Ascanius founded the city of Alba Longa in the hills to the south of today's Rome. It became the "mother city" of Rome, and was the birthplace of a legendary pair of twins ...

The twins Romulus (left) and Remus, mythical founders of Rome; a marble relief from imperial Rome.

The Capitoline she-wolf suckles the two boys Romulus and Remus – for a long time this sculpture was believed to date from the Etruscan era.

Romulus and Remus

When Numitor, king of Alba Longa, was overthrown by his brother Amulius, the usurper forced Numitor's daughter to become a priestess in the temple of Vesta. As a vestal virgin, she was pledged to chastity, so under "normal" conditions would not be able to bear any descendants, who could later challenge Amulius for the throne. But the god of war, Mars, was so incensed by the brazen usurper that he forced his way into the temple of Vesta and made Rhea Silvia pregnant. When she gave birth to twin sons, Amulius commanded that the boys be drowned in the Tiber. But the boat-shaped cradle in which Romulus and Remus were launched was washed up on the shore. A she-wolf looked after the babies, protecting and suckling them until they were discovered by a shepherd, who then brought them up. When the twins came of age, they killed the usurper and restored their grandfather to power. The Roman historian Livy (59 BC–AD 17) wrote that the twin brothers wanted to found a city at the place where they had been abandoned. Romulus made his way to a hill, now called the Palatine Hill; Remus went to another, now called the Aventine. Whichever one of them saw the most birds in

flight, they agreed, would be the victor in the contest between the two rival brothers to see who would rule the newly founded city.

Remus saw six vultures, and a little later Romulus saw 12. This had fatal consequences for the loser, who could not accept his defeat that easily. Livy gave two versions of what happened next: in one version, there was a violent fight, in which Remus was "knocked down in the tumult". According to the other, better-known, version, Remus apparently jumped mockingly over his brother's new walls and was then killed by the incensed Romulus, with the words: "This is what will happen in future to anyone who jumps over the walls of the city!"

The mysterious she-wolf

It seems reasonable to doubt the historical accuracy of the *fama*, as Livy calls the legend in the Latin original. Livy thought it was possible that the mother of the twins had been raped but felt it was more "noble" to claim that Mars was the father of her children. In addition, many believed that the wife of the shepherd was called "she-wolf" because she gave her body without discrimination. Livy took this to be the real "origin of the wonderful legend".

Whatever scraps of truth may lie behind the legend of Rome's beginnings, the city went on to become one of the founding cities of Western civilization and play a significant role in the long history of Christianity.

Poetry and truth

Archeological excavations have shown that there were hut settlements on several of the "seven hills" of Rome in the Iron Age. The oldest was on the Palatine Hill. It is possible that in around 753 BC – the year to which Livy dates the foundation of the city – the individual settlements joined together into a community. The hills were not high, but here, at the intersection of ancient trade routes, mainly transporting salt, they were strategically significant. At the point where the city gradually grew up, the island in the Tiber now known as the Isola Tiberina, helped form a useful crossing point over the river. The island has its own legend, which says that Rome's citizens threw the

Iron Age: model of a hut on the Palatine Hill.

body of the tyrant Tarquinius Superbus into the river, where silt gradually accumulated around it until it became an island.

But the raw facts cannot compare to the more vibrant myths. Perhaps it's best to go along with a common Italian saying: "*Se non è vero, è ben trovato*" – "If it's not true, at least it's a good story".

The eternal myth of the foundation of Rome: Romulus and Remus abandoned on the banks of the Tiber, in a contemporary setting (engraving by Matthäus Merian the Elder, 1630).

As seen by artists (from left): Numa Pompilius, Rome's second king, with the nymph Egeria (painted by Angelica Kauffmann, 1794); Tullus Hostilius, the third king, in battle (Giuseppe Cesari, 16th/17th century); Tarquinius Priscus, the fifth king, is killed (Matthäus Merian the Elder, 1630); Tarquinius Sextus, a son of Tarquinius Superbus, rapes Lucretia, a Roman woman, who subsequently kills herself (Tintoretto, 1559).

753 BC
Legendary date of the foundation of Rome by Romulus, who is the first king (c. 753–715 BC).

7th century BC
The legend of the rape of the Sabine women; proof that, from its early days, Rome formed alliances with other nations.

Around 715–673 BC
The reign of King Numa Pompilius, a Sabine, who introduces the 12-month calendar.

659 BC
Under Tullus Hostilius, Alba Longa is conquered and destroyed.

About 640 BC
During the reign of Ancus Marcius, grandson of Numa Pompilius, the port of Ostia is founded.

616 BC
Tarquinius Priscus is the first of the Etruscan rulers of Rome.

565 BC
King Servius orders the construction of city walls named after him.

534 BC
King Servius is killed. His successor is Tarquinius Superbus.

509 BC
Tarquinius Superbus is overthrown as a result of his despotic rule.

After 509 BC
Rome becomes a republic, headed by two consuls (until 27 BC).

Fist-fighters: this Greek amphora, found in a town to the north-west of Rome, shows that there were close links between Greece and the Etruscan Cerveteri.

The Etruscans

The rule of the Roman kings began with Romulus. Livy narrated that Romulus declared his "city" – which is probably best imagined as a collection of small villages – to be an asylum, a refuge for all those who were wandering the country, homeless for whatever reason (most had done something wrong and were on the run). The unification of separate tribes into a larger community was first brought about by the Etruscans, who came from the area north of Rome. Today, it is widely accepted that the city got its name not from its legendary founder but from the Etruscan ruling dynasty, the Ruma. It was extremely advantageous for the development of the city that the Etruscans, who were based in the area that is now Tuscany, brought Rome under their control. Rome first blossomed under the Etruscan kings. Among other things,

they introduced drainage and water supply systems, some of which still survive, and the construction of Roman houses was strongly influenced by standard Etruscan methods. Certain traditional ceremonies can also be traced back to this time: gladiator fights are of Etruscan origin, as are circus games and the custom of building a triumphal arch for victorious commanders.

The Etruscan belief system comprised a pantheon of gods and goddesses, who represented the world they saw around them. Tivr was god of the moon, Cathan and Usil the sun, while Turan was the goddess of love and Leinth the goddess of death. The Etruscans believed in an afterlife and consulted their deities at every turn, as did the Romans who succeeded them.

Rome became the focal point of power for the whole region, partly because rival cities such as Alba Longa – its own "mother city" – were destroyed by the Romans. One indication that the Romans were turning their covetous eyes further afield was the creation of the sea port of Ostia in around 600 BC.

Plebeians and patricians

The growth of the population and the expansion of the city's sphere of influence demanded more than just structural developments. A "constitution" was also needed to establish the hierarchical order and define individual areas of responsibility. The king was sup-

Vivid frescoes: the Tomb of the Leopards (6th–2nd century BC) in the Etruscan necropolis of Tarquinia.

Cult of the dead: this Tomb of the Priests (6th–2nd century BC) is also in Tarquinia.

Rape of the virgins

There were apparently few women among the shady characters who flooded into Rome in its early days – the excess numbers of men gave rise to the worry that Rome would only last a generation due to a lack of descendants. To prevent this, so legend has it, a feast was arranged, to which the Romans invited many families from the Sabines, tribes from the area surrounding Rome. At the height of the feast, the Romans attacked the guests and drove them all away – except the young women, whom they held captive and kept for themselves …

In the next part of the legend the Sabines attacked Rome, but the women, now married to Romans, positioned themselves among the fighting men and intervened in the battle, pointing out that they now all belonged to the same family – some as their fathers, others as their husbands – so why fight each other? It seems that the story does have a kernel of truth: the Romans and Sabines apparently coexisted peacefully in the 6th century BC, and even formed alliances at times.

The Rape of the Sabine women has provided a potent inspiration for many works of art, particularly in the Renaissance. The "rape" was not the act of sexual violation by which we understand the word today, but rather a kidnapping of the women in order to ensure the continuity and survival of the new city. Many artists through the ages have portrayed the story, from Nicolas

Giambologna's magnificent *Rape of the Sabine Women* (16th century).

Poussin and Peter Paul Rubens to Pablo Picasso.

ported by senators, who came from the ranks of rich landowners; they called themselves patricians (sons of noble "fathers", or *patres*). This was a relatively small group compared to the large mass of plebeians – tradesmen, workers, merchants, traders, and small farmers – who had some rights, but were excluded from most forms of office.

As Etruscan-style ideas of kingship gained ground, the distance between the ruler and his subjects increased. The last of the Etruscan kings took the idea of his supremacy too far. This king, Tarquinius, was given the epithet Superbus, which means proud or arrogant. He wantonly disregarded the laws of the city, which eventually led to him being overthrown, and he, his children, and his whole dynasty were banned from Rome for ever: an early example of the truth of the saying "Pride comes before a fall".

After the last king was driven out, Rome became a republic – a long period of social tensions, internal power struggles, and wars with foreign opponents. Great figures of this era included (from left): the commander Scipio and his opponent, the Carthaginian general Hannibal, in the 3rd century BC; in the last days of the republic (1st century BC) the powerful politicians Pompey, Crassus, Caesar, and his friend – and murderer – Brutus.

499 BC
The republic of Rome is at war with the Latins.

396 BC
The Etruscan city of Veii is conquered. Rome starts to become the predominant power in the region.

390 BC
Rome is captured by Gauls and only released on payment of a ransom.

264–146 BC
Three Punic wars: Rome fights the rival power of Carthage, which is finally crushed in 146 BC.

168 BC
Rome gains control of Greece after the Macedonian War.

133 BC
Tiberius Gracchus becomes tribune of the people: battles between the Senate and the people.

Around 100 BC
Civil war between aristocrats, under Sulla, and democrats, led by Marius.

71 BC
Slave uprising, led by Spartacus, is defeated.

60 BC
The triumvirate of Caesar, Crassus, and Pompey rule.

51 BC
Caesar conquers Gaul.

44 BC
Caesar, dictator since the year 46 BC, is murdered.

31 BC
Octavian rules Rome.

Myths depicted centuries later – the consul Publius Decius Mus (died 340 BC) prophesies the victory of the Romans over the Latins (painting by Peter Paul Rubens, around 1617).

Caesar and the last years of the republic

Small farmers suffered from the many wars, as soldiers were recruited from their ranks. Their land lay fallow and they were often forced to sell to large landowners, who had sufficient slaves to be able to continue to farm profitably. This resulted in the formation of a new social class, whose members had served

In 60 BC, a triumvirate of three men – Pompey, Crassus, and Caesar – effectively held all political power. Crassus, notorious for having crushed the slave rebellion led by Spartacus, was one of the richest men in Rome. He was killed attempting to conquer Parthia, the empire that included modern-day Iran. The best known of the three is Gaius Julius Caesar, who became consul in that year.

Off to Italy: Hannibal's feared weapons were his legendary war elephants (fresco from the early 16th century).

A new power

After driving out the last king of the Etruscan dynasty, no successor was appointed; instead, Rome became a republic. From the year 509 BC, instead of a single ruler, power was in the hands of two consuls, who monitored each other and whose period in office was limited to one year. These two officials came from the patrician class – the nobility who appointed all high officials. In later times, the plebeians – the ordinary people – frequently protested against this supremacy of a relatively small class.

"Hannibal is at the gates"

The strengthening of the state structure made expansion possible. Rome waged war on the Etruscans, who were crushingly defeated in 396 BC. Six years later, however, Brennus, a Gaulish chief, conquered Rome and released it only after he had been paid a large ransom. The saying Vae victis (woe to the vanquished) is attributed to him.
Rome's great rival in the Mediterranean was the naval

power of Carthage, capital city of the Phoenicians, in present-day Tunisia. In 509 BC, the Romans signed a trade agreement with the Phoenicians, but just over 200 years later any attempt at peaceful coexistence was abandoned. Between 264 and 241 BC, the First Punic War raged (the Carthaginians were also known as Punics). It ended in the surrender of Carthage, which lost control of Sicily: the island became the first Roman province. In 218 BC, clashes flared up again. Carthage's commander Hannibal inflicted heavy losses on the Romans; but despite the legendary cry of horror "Hannibal ante portas" ("Hannibal is at the gates"), the Carthaginians did not manage to capture the city. In 201 BC, Carthage had to admit defeat. In 149 BC, the city was flattened by an earthquake; the surviving inhabitants were sold into slavery, and the Punic lands became Rome's African province.
One of the great generals of antiquity, Hannibal's legendary status was cemented by his extraordinary achievement of crossing the Pyrenees and the Alps to enter northern Italy with an army that included war elephants.

"Et tu, Brute?" The murder of Gaius Julius Caesar on 15 March 44 BC by his opponents (painting by Friedrich Heinrich Füger, 1815).

in the wars and now wanted to have political influence; at the same time, impoverished small farmers streamed into Rome in vast numbers. There they soon formed a sort of urban proletariat, and this social issue threatened to upset the whole structure of the state. A bloody civil war flared up, and several slave uprisings increased social instability.

He went on to conquer Gaul and successfully defended the republic against the Teutons, who were pushing south. In 49 BC, he waged a civil war against Pompey, his former ally. This war ended in Caesar's victory, and from then on he ruled alone, as dictator – until he was murdered in 44 BC by supporters of the old republican system, including his friend Brutus.

After a period of confusion and civil war, a desire emerged in Rome for a single, authoritarian ruler, but one who would leave the republican structures intact. From left: Octavian, a great-nephew of Caesar, became the first emperor, Augustus, in 27 BC; his successors in the 1st to 3rd centuries included Nero, Trajan and Marcus Aurelius; Constantine I promoted Christianity in the 4th century.

27 BC
Octavian becomes Emperor Augustus. End of the civil wars.

About AD 30
Jesus of Nazareth is crucified in the province of Judea.

42
The apostle Peter arrives in Rome. Christianity finds many followers.

64
The great fire in Rome and the persecution of Christians under Nero.

Around 60–65
The apostles Peter and Paul are killed.

98
Trajan becomes the first non-Roman emperor.

117–138
Emperor Hadrian travels throughout the empire.

161
Marcus Aurelius, the "philosopher-emperor", comes to power.

293
Diocletian divides the empire into four.

324
Under Constantine the Great, Rome is divided into east and west.

391
Christianity becomes the state religion of Rome.

410
The Visigoths, led by King Alarich, plunder Rome.

Life in ancient Rome

Trajan's Baths, and the reconstruction of the Domus Flavia (above) on the Palatine Hill, illustrate the magnificent display of urban wealth in ancient Rome.

The top strata of Roman society were the patricians who could trace their ancestry to one of the 100 patriarchs, or founders of the city. Below them came the plebeians, free-born citizens, then the freedmen (freed slaves), and finally the slaves. Life in the capital of the Roman Empire in many respects must have been similar to life in large European cities such as London at the start of the industrial age. The *domus* – which varied in degrees of magnificence – was the palatial residence of one family and its slaves. For the lower classes there were *insulae* – tenement houses with shops and workshops on the ground floor, and modest to poor living quarters on the upper floors. Fires often broke out in these lower class districts, and a fire service, the *vigiles*, was founded to fight fire in any way they could – water generally had to be transported by hand in leather buckets. The *vigiles* had other responsibilities as well: crime was a problem – there were times when well-heeled Romans would only go out at night in a litter, accompanied by armed slaves.

Imperial and impressive – how Emperor Domitian's Palace on the Palatine Hill might have looked in the 3rd century.

Pax Romana

After centuries of domestic political turmoil, a long period of stability dawned under Octavian, a great-nephew of Caesar, who became emperor and was given the title "Augustus" – this was the time of *Pax Romana* (also known as *Pax Augusta*, the peace of Augustus). However, foreign wars continued as before, particularly against the Germanic tribes. The province of Judea, although it had been conquered by Pompey in 63 BC, remained a major trouble spot, which is why the prefect Pontius Pilate took draconian measures when a man called Jesus of Nazareth, preaching about love and forgiveness, found numerous followers there: it was feared that a spiritual movement could become a political one.

"Queen of Cities"

A striking number of Augustus' successors were either

The Ara Pacis Augustae, the Altar of Peace, was a symbol of the change in the nation's policies under Emperor Augustus.

killed or committed suicide. Caligula (emperor between 37 and 41) was the first victim of megalomania – a mixture of delusions of grandeur and persecution mania, often expressed in the megalomaniac's conviction of their own divinity. Nero (emperor in the years 54–68) is considered the perfect example of a megalomaniac ruler.

In 98, the Spaniard Trajan became emperor; in the hands of this experienced and capable officer, the empire reached its prime. The philosopher-emperor Marcus Aurelius (161–180) wrote *Meditations*, full of wisdom and insight – in practical terms he showed himself to be less clear-minded: going against tradition, he made his inept son his successor. The military emperor Caracalla (211–217) unleashed a regime of building activity that the capital had not seen since the time of Augustus. Emperor Aurelian (270–275) again sought to strengthen the empire; emperor Diocletian (284–305) reacted strongly against revolt within the empire, justifying his position as absolute monarch. Emperor Constantine (306–337) reversed Diocletian's policies of hate and persecution, and granted Christians full religious equality under an edict of tolerance; he founded a second capital in Constantinople (today's Istanbul). The city on the Bosphorus soon began to outstrip the city on the Tiber as the "Queen of Cities".

Under Theodosius (379–395), Christianity was declared the state religion. Constantinople, also called East Rome, became the capital of the Byzantine Empire, which lasted until 1453, when it was conquered by the Turks. The West Roman Empire, on the other hand, continued to decline, and the last emperor, Romulus, was overthrown and driven out by the German commander Odoaker in 476.

Trajan's Column, dating from the 2nd century, has bands of reliefs, about 200 m (650 feet) long in total, arranged in a spiral. They show the conquest of Dacia by Emperor Trajan.

"The Pope is the perpetual and visible principle and foundation of unity in multiplicity", for bishops as for all believers, as
stated in the Dogmatic Constitution on the Church of the
Second Vatican Council (1962–65). Jesus of Nazareth is considered the supreme example of that religious office. Distinguished medieval popes (from left): Anastasius II (5th century);
Gregory VII (11th century); and Innocent III (13th century).

476
The last emperor, Romu-
lus, is overthrown.

568
Invasion by the Germanic
Lombards. Rome is offi-
cially part of the Byzan-
tine Empire.

590–604
Under Gregory I, the
papacy gains more power
and influence.

752
Stephen II asks Pepin,
king of the Franks, for aid
against the Lombards. The
Church is given extensive
territories under the
Donation of Pepin (754).

800
The Frankish king Charle-
magne is crowned Holy
Roman Emperor by Pope
Leo III.

962
The German king Otto I is
crowned emperor by John
XII; Otto orders that the
pope can only be elected
with the agreement of the
emperor.

1057
Stephen IX is elected pope
without the consent of
the emperor.

1122
The "investiture contro-
versy" between the pope
and the emperor over the
appointment of bishops is
settled, with compromises
on both sides.

1309
Pope Clement V moves his
residence from Rome to
Avignon in France.

Representative of Jesus

Rome's prominent role in the
Roman Catholic religion can
be traced back to St Peter,
one of the chosen disciples
of Jesus. According to Christian tradition, appointed by
Jesus to be his successor and
representative on earth,
Peter became the first bishop
of Rome. He was martyred
around AD 64 – crucified
head down on the orders of
Nero who sought to blame
the Christians for the Great
Fire of Rome.
The early Christians had carried out their rites and ceremonies in secret, but after
the edict on tolerance was
issued by Emperor Constantine the first public Christian
buildings were constructed.
The first St Peter's was begun
in around 324; work started
on Santa Maria Maggiore in

**Supreme symbol of faith:
the reliquary with the
chains of St Peter is kept
in the Basilica of San Pietro
in Vincoli.**

356, and on Santa Sabina in
422. Siricius (384–399) was
the first Roman bishop to
give himself the title "papa",
meaning father, which is the
origin of the word "pope".

The keys to salvation: the baroque statue of St Peter in
front of St Peter's Basilica points the way to believers from
around the world.

Roman Catholics

While Rome continued to
lose its importance as the
focal point of political power
from the early 4th century
onward, it simultaneously
developed into the most

important place in the world
for Christians, after the holy
city of Jerusalem. The holders
of the Holy See asserted
themselves not only in their
role as spiritual leaders of
the followers of the Christian
faith, but also increasingly

developed and expanded their political power.

In 754, the – Catholic – king of the Franks, Pepin III, granted the Church extensive territories on the Italian peninsula. These formed the physical foundation for the Papal States, which over the course of centuries extended as far as Tuscany in the north and almost to Naples in the south. In 1075, Gregory VII announced the *Dictatus Papae*, asserting that the spiritual and political powers of the pope exceeded that of any other Christian – including the emperor. The

(1198–1216) and Rome flourished. However, in 1309 Pope Clement V, a Frenchman, moved the papal seat to Avignon and thus into the sphere of influence of the kings of France – a temporary triumph for secular power.

In 1377, Gregory XI brought the papacy back to Rome, but the intervening decades, when Rome was not the sole seat of the leaders of Christianity, had had serious consequences for the city. The population had fallen, as had many buildings. Grass grew in the streets, and sheep and

Santa Maria in Trastevere is probably the oldest of all the churches dedicated to the Virgin and was the first site in Rome where Christians could worship in public.

so-called investiture controversy that followed involving the secular leaders and the leaders of the Church was finally settled in 1122 with the Concordat of Worms. Theocracy reached its peak in the papacy of Innocent III

goats grazed in the heart of the city.

Gregory I (Gregory the Great) was an important pope in the 6th century (15th C. fresco by Andrea Delitio, in Atri cathedral).

The tomb of Pope Sixtus IV in St Peter's in Rome (right). Sixtus' term of office (1471–84) is considered to be the start of the Renaissance papacy, characterized by an extravagant court and shameless nepotism. This was one of the reasons why Christian leaders throughout Europe called for the reform of the Roman Catholic Church; eventually this resulted in the Protestant Reformation, led by Martin Luther.

1377
Gregory XI moves the papacy back to Rome from Avignon.

1378–1417
The great schism in the Church: two popes rule simultaneously, in Rome and Avignon.

1447
Nicholas V founds the Vatican library.

1477
Work starts on the Sistine Chapel, under Sixtus IV.

1504
Julius II brings Michelangelo to Rome, to design his tomb.

1506
The foundation stone is laid for the construction of the new St Peter's, to designs by Bramante.

1508
Michelangelo starts decorating the vaulted ceiling of the Sistine Chapel.

1509
Raphael starts on the frescoes in the *stanze*, the private chambers of Julius II.

1510/11
Martin Luther visits Rome; he vehemently criticizes the situation he finds there, especially the selling of indulgences.

1527
Sack of Rome: the city is plundered by soldiers of the emperor Charles V. Pope Clement VII takes refuge in the Castel Sant'-Angelo.

A pugnacious pope

The foundation stone for the new St Peter's was laid in 1506 by Pope Julius II (1443–1513, pope from 1502). Critics maintained that he only commissioned such a huge building in order for there to be room in it for the grandiose tomb designed for him by Michelangelo. In the event, the tomb was not quite as monumental as originally planned, and space was found for it in a church of rather more modest dimensions, San Pietro in Vincoli.

Julius II went down in history not only as a patron of the arts, but also as a successful commander. He won back territories for the Papal States, and "founded a power that was never before possessed by a pope", according to the historian Leopold von Ranke.

Artist and patron: Michelangelo in discussion with Pope Julius II (painting, A. Fontebuoni).

The recumbent figure on the tomb of Pope Julius II (main picture) was created by Maso del Bosco.

The power of the popes

After his return from exile in Avignon in 1377, Gregory XI and his followers set about reviving Rome's former magnificence. The passion for ostentation of some popes knew no limits. As the Church now had enormous wealth, its leaders could employ the most important artists of their time. To decorate the Sistine Chapel – named after himself – Pope Sixtus IV brought to Rome the painters Pinturicchio,

Perugino, and Signorelli from Umbria, and Botticelli, Ghirlandaio, Cosimo Roselli, and Piero di Cosimo from Florence. Later, the great Michelangelo was commissioned – by Julius II – to paint the ceiling of the chapel with the now-world-famous frescoes, while Raphael decorated the pope's private chambers in the Vatican.

The reconstruction of St Peter's was the greatest project of its type for

plan that encountered a great deal of resistance. In order to finance the costly new building, believers were allowed to buy "indulgences", a remission of the punishment for sin, which – in addition to the worldliness of the popes – was one of the reasons that Martin Luther demanded a reformation of the Church.

Paradoxically, further magnificent buildings were constructed during the Counter-Reformation – the papal

became entangled in the wars between France and Spain for supremacy in northern Italy, hoping to profit by them and be able to gain new territories. In 1527, Spanish soldiers and German mercenaries conquered Rome, plundered, and slaughtered the inhabitants. The pope took refuge in the Castel Sant'Angelo; but of the 55,000 or so people who lived in Rome at that time, about 33,000 were killed or abducted, or fled.

A grandiose effect, ingeniously staged. The dome of St Peter's was designed by the great Michelangelo.

Michelangelo's frescoes in the Sistine Chapel.

An eye-catching institution – the Swiss Guard.

decades. Pope Julius II commissioned the architect Donato Bramante to tear down the old basilica, built in the 4th century on the site of the tomb of St Peter, and to construct a new one, a

reaction to the efforts of Luther – in order to show all believers the unbroken power of the Catholic Church.

There was a cruel setback to the development of the city when Pope Clement VII

The Sack of Rome on 6 May 1527 is remembered every year when new recruits to the Swiss Guard, the soldiers who guard the Vatican and the pope, are sworn in on 6 May.

forces of the Papal States. The guards must be Catholic single males aged between 19 and 30, with Swiss citizenship, who have trained with the Swiss military and have an exemplary service record.

The age of baroque was another brilliant period of art in Rome. From left: The extravagant Pope Urban VIII, an admirer of the great architect and sculptor Gianlorenzo Bernini (1598–1680), commissioned many works from the artist; Bernini is buried in the church of Santa Maria Maggiore; Innocent X was pope from 1644 until 1655, and broke with his predecessors' tradition of nepotism.

1540
Recognition of the Jesuit Order by Paul III.

1582
Sixtus V commissions lavish redesigns of many squares in Rome during the Counter-Reformation.

1600
Giordano Bruno is burned as a heretic in the Campo de' Fiori.

1626
Official opening of the new St Peter's (the foundation stone was laid in 1506).

1631
The Papal States reach their greatest extent under Urban VIII.

1633
Galileo Galilei, condemned to death as a heretic, retracts his "blasphemous" teaching.

1656
The plague kills around 15,000 people in Rome. The colonnades of St Peter's Square are built to designs by Bernini.

1726
The Spanish Steps are built, to designs by Francesco de Sanctis.

1763
German Johann Joachim Winckelmann becomes the papal supervisor of all Roman antiquities.

1786
German poet Goethe lives in Rome (not continuously) until 1788.

Giordano Bruno

Bruno – an intellectual who would later influence the spiritual life of Europe – was born in Nola, near Naples, in 1548. He entered the Dominican Order at a young age, but left, accused of heresy, and wandered through Europe. In Venice, he fell into the hands of the Inquisition and was taken to

The memorial in the Campo de' Fiori to the monk and philosopher Giordano Bruno, whose pantheistic ideas were to influence such important literary figures as Spinoza, Herder, and Goethe.

Rome. He was imprisoned for more than seven years, and was burnt at the stake on 17 February 1600. Giordano Bruno, who equated God with nature, did not consider himself an atheist in any way, but he held the view that God was present everywhere: "In the universe, there is no difference between the finite and the infinite, the greatest and the smallest".

A baroque view of life – the ceiling painting *The Triumph of Divine Providence* by Pietro da Cortona (1596–1669), in the Palazzo Barberini, served to glorify Pope Urban VIII and his family.

Heretics and believers

The flurry of building activity in Rome under Pope Sixtus V (1585–90) continued into the 17th century. Above all, the reason behind the magnificent, newly constructed churches was – in the opinion of the Holy See – to display the triumph of the true faith over heresy. If the

A changing city

In 1631, under Urban VIII, the Papal States reached their greatest point of expansion. In Gianlorenzo Bernini the pope found an ingenious architect and sculptor, who understood the pope's plans to make the heart of Christianity even more impressive. Bernini created, among many other works, the Fountain of

Gianlorenzo Bernini

Born in Naples in 1598, Giovanni Lorenzo (Gianlorenzo) Bernini came to Rome in 1606 and was soon "discovered" by Pope Paul V. A brilliant architect and sculptor, Bernini made his exceptional mark on the baroque face of Rome, working for eight popes, until his death in the year 1680.

Death of a believer: Bernini's masterpiece *The Blessed Lodovica Albertoni* in the church of San Francesco a Ripa.

The glory of God and His representatives: the design and execution of Bernini's tomb of Pope Urban VIII (in St Peter's).

power of imagery could not achieve this end, then deviation from the official line could also be addressed in different ways: in 1600, a monk named Giordano Bruno, who had questioned, among other things, that the earth was the hub of the universe, was burned to death in the Campo de' Fiori. Astronomer Galileo Galilei (1564–1642), who made similar supposedly heretical assertions, escaped death at the Inquisition's stake because, unlike Giordano Bruno, he retracted his theses when faced with the prospect of execution.

the Four Rivers in Piazza Navona and the *Ecstasy of St Teresa*, a statue in Santa Maria della Vittoria; he also completed the colonnaded walk around St Peter's Square. The architect Francesco Borromini was a friendly rival of Bernini. In the high baroque period, the Piazza Navona was given its final layout, the Spanish Steps were laid, and the Trevi Fountain was constructed. The engraver Gianbattista Piranesi recorded the changing image of the city in his *Vedute di Roma antica e moderna* (Scenes of Rome, ancient and modern).

Ornate canopy: Bernini's bronze baldachin for the papal altar in St Peter's is 29 m (95 feet) high.

From left: In 1798, Napoleon's troops occupied Rome – a short interlude; Giuseppe Mazzini (1805–1872) and Camillo Benso, Count of Cavour (1810–1861), had a formative influence on the struggle for the unification of Italy; King Victor Emmanuel II (ruled 1861–78) gave Cavour a free hand in the politics of unification; the name of Pius IX (pope from 1846 to 1878) has always been associated with the dogma of papal infallibility.

1798
After the capture by Napoleon's troops, a republic is proclaimed in Rome, and Pope Pius VI is forced to flee the city.

1800
The pope's successor, Pius VII, is elected in Venice.

1801
Pius VII signs a treaty with France and returns to Rome.

1808
Rome remains occupied by the French, and the pope is again exiled.

From 1820
Many efforts to unify the Italian states.

1848
Nationalist uprising in Rome; Pius IX, who opposed the unification of Italy, has to flee.

1849
Pius IX returns to power with the help of the French.

1860
The Papal States now consist only of the city of Rome and a strip of land in Lazio, also known as Latium.

1861
King Victor Emmanuel II is proclaimed ruler of all of Italy.

1870
The king's troops storm Rome and end the pope's rule.

Goethe in Rome

Drawn like a magnet to Rome, Johann Wolfgang von Goethe stayed in the Eternal City from November 1786 until February 1787, and then from June 1787 until April 1788. He lived with the painter Johann Heinrich Wilhelm Tischbein on the Corso. Here he worked on *Torquato Tasso* and *Egmont* and wrote: "We go back and forth enthusiastically; I am getting to know the plans of the old and new Rome, look-

Goethe in Rome – drawing by J.H.W. Tischbein.

ing at ruins and buildings, visiting one villa or another; the greatest curiosities are being dealt with slowly, I'm just keeping my eyes open, walking and looking and going back, because you can only prepare yourself for Rome in Rome". The poet was impressed with Rome, as the following sentence, noted after a walk across the Protestant cemetery, confirms: "Oh, to lie here: that would be beautiful, and infinitely more beautiful than living in Germany".

Napoleon's legacy

In 1798, Rome was captured by the French emperor Napoleon and a republic was proclaimed. After the turmoil of the Napoleonic era calls for the unification of the country became stronger throughout Italy. The Corsican had broken down many of the long-established systems of rule and the leaders of numerous small states and city states were deposed. Many Italians now yearned for a united Italy, one that could hold its own among the other strong European nations.

conservative position of Pope Pius IX in matters of both faith and politics led to him being expelled from Rome. Although Giuseppe Garibaldi, the leader of the republican freedom movement, supposedly announced "*O Roma o morte*" – "Rome or death" – he was unable to hold the city and in 1849 Pius IX returned to the Vatican. The Nationalists finally

Giuseppe Garibaldi

Born on 4 July 1807 in Nice, Giuseppe Garibaldi was the son of a fisherman. He joined the Giovane Italia (Young Italy) movement in 1833 and after taking part in an unsuccessful uprising, he was condemned to death by a Piedmontese court in 1834, after which he fled to South America via France. In the revolutionary year of 1848, he made his return to Italy, and in February 1849 led the fight against the French.

The Expedition of the Thousand, famously led by Garibaldi, is legendary – a revolutionary adventure that started in the night of 5 May 1860 with the capture of two

steamships in the port of Genoa. Five days later, the rebels landed on the westernmost point of the island of Sicily. From there, they conquered the island and then moved to the mainland, where Garibaldi took his place next to King Victor Emmanuel II in Naples on 7 September. This became the turning point in the formation of a united kingdom of Italy.

However, Garibaldi's revolutionary impetuosity brought him into conflict with his former allies, and in spite of many attempts he failed to achieve his greatest goal, the march on Rome. He died on 2 June 1882 on the island of Caprera.

Il Vittoriano commemorates the first king of Italy.

Astride his steed: Italy's national hero Garibaldi.

"*O Roma o morte*"

Some of the most stubborn opponents of unification over the next half-century were the popes, who saw that their own power – secular power in this case – was threatened. The extremely

Il Vittoriano, the memorial to Victor Emmanuel II on the Piazza Venezia, has attractive details – but as a whole, many Romans and tourists find it too large and bombastic.

conquered Rome in 1870, after bitter defensive fighting by the papal troops. And so the secular leadership of the popes ended after more than a thousand years. Though not forbidden to travel, Pius IX declared himself "a prisoner" and in order not to be seen to be accepting of the authority of the new Italian government in any way, refused to leave the Vatican. He outlived his opponent Victor Emmanuel II by one month, dying in February 1878.

Symbolic of the narrow divide between art and kitsch: Garibaldi with the personifications of the cities of Venice and Rome, a 19th-century painting (Museo del Risorgimento).

The cultural achievements of the Rome of recent times is famed throughout the world. From left: Great writer Alberto Moravia (1907–1990); legendary film star Claudia Cardinale (born 1938); and world-famous composer of film music Ennio Morricone (born 1928); Silvia Venturini Fendi (born 1960) is a successful fashion designer; Cecilia Bartoli (born 1966) is a celebrated mezzosoprano; Eros Ramazzotti (born 1963) is a rock star.

1871
Rome becomes the capital of a united Italy.

1922
Fascist march on Rome; Benito Mussolini becomes prime minister.

1929
Mussolini and the Holy See sign the Lateran Pact.

1937
Mussolini initiates the foundation of Cinecittà, because he wants to exploit film for propaganda purposes.

1943
Some parts of Rome are seriously damaged by Allied bombers.

1944
Rome is liberated on 4 June by US and British troops.

1946
Abolition of the monarchy, proclamation of the Republic of Italy.

1957
The Treaties of Rome form the foundation for the European Economic Community.

1960
The Olympic Games are held in Rome.

1962
Pope John XXIII calls the Second Vatican Council.

2005
Pope John Paul II dies; he is succeeded by Cardinal Joseph Ratzinger as Benedict XVI.

The talking statue

The story goes that a tailor called Pasquino, who lived in Rome in the 15th century, was well known for his sharp-tongued comments on current affairs – even the rulers of the time were often the subject of his satirical verses. In 1501, during digging work at the edge of the Piazza Navona, an ancient statue was found that was so badly damaged that no collector was interested in acquiring it; this torso was simply leaned against the wall of a *palazzo*. The people called it the Pasquino statue, and it soon became the custom to stick notes on it at night, on which were written critical, and sometimes malicious, remarks

The Pasquino statue, a safety-valve for discontent.

about political decisions. Over time, this custom was forgotten, but it was revived when Hitler visited Mussolini in Rome in 1938. When Silvio Berlusconi became prime minister for the first time in 1994, it is said that a particularly large number of comments were found on Pasquino. The origins of the Italian word *pasquill* (lampoon) apparently can be traced back to this statue.

The Roman question

From 1861, Italy was a united country headed by a king, Victor Emmanuel II, from the House of Savoy. Rome became the capital in 1871 – however, the Lombards, Tuscans, and Piedmontese expressed doubts and wondered whether Milan, Florence, or Turin would not have made a better *capitale d'Italia*. For the fascists, who came to power after World War I, there was no doubt: for them, Rome was an embodiment of the mighty ancient empire, the classical

A milestone for the Italian film industry: Anna Magnani in Roberto Rossellini's classic *Rome, Open City* (1945).

world power, and the supporters of the self-styled *Duce*, Benito Mussolini, attempted to link themselves with this past glory.
In 1922, Mussolini organized a protest march, with marchers converging on the capital from all directions, in which about 26,000 of his supporters took part – he himself took the sleeper train. The ruler at the time, King Victor Emmanuel III, appointed Mussolini prime minister.

In 1929, Mussolini solved the so-called Roman question, which referred to the relationship between the Church and state, and thus also the status of Rome: in the Lateran Pact, it was agreed that in future the pope would be the leader of an independent Vatican State. This *Stato della Città del Vaticano*, covering an area of just 44 hectares (108 acres), was all that remained of the once powerful Papal States. To celebrate the "reconciliation", Mussolini had the Via della Conciliazione built, sacrificing a large section of the medieval Borgo, between the Vatican and the Tiber. In 1937, the fascist leader, who had discovered that film was a useful medium for propaganda, founded the Cinecittà film studios; in the same year, he had numerous medieval buildings torn down, including about 20 churches, to make way for a World Exhibition planned for 1942 (Esposizione Universale di Roma, shortened to EUR). On the site, he constructed the

Victor Emmanuel III's indecisive position towards fascism, and in 1946 the Italians decided in a referendum to abolish the monarchy and form a republic. For administrative reasons, the country was divided into regions. Rome was not only the capital of the Italian Republic, but also the administrative heart of the region of Lazio. The city also naturally remained the seat of the pope. So today Rome is no longer the capital of the world – *caput mundi* – but continues to be a triple capital. Although Catholicism is no longer the official Italian

Screen star Monica Bellucci greets her fans.

The metro

Rome's underground train network has just two lines, called A and B. A third line, Linea C, running from north to south-east, from Grottarossa to Pantano, has long been planned. But the start of building work has continually been delayed, for the same reason that makes most new-build projects in the inner city very problematical: evidence of ancient culture and historical buildings are at risk of being irretrievably lost. The digging work for the new Linea C therefore has to be carried out at the same time as scientifically supervised archeological excavations. Near to the Imperial Forums, there is now an underground

A journey on the Roman underground.

Pictures that touch everyone: Rome has hosted the annual *Festa internazionale di Roma* film festival since 2006.

Palazzo della Civiltà del Lavoro, whose architecture echoed classical forms but was popularly known as the "square Colosseum". However, the Exhibition did not take place because of World War II, which Italy entered on 19 July 1940.

During the war, Rome experienced Allied bombing on a number of occasions. The San Lorenzo quarter suffered devastating damage, but on the whole the city emerged

fairly unscathed, certainly in comparison with many other European cities. After several attempts, Pius XII had Rome declared an open city – enabling enemy troops to enter without resistance, thereby protecting the city, its treasure, and its inhabitants from further harm. On 4 June 1944, Rome was liberated by the advancing Allied troops.

The monarchy had fallen into disrepute because of King

state religion (a concordat was signed between the state and the Vatican in 1984), the Eternal City remains the focal point of belief for more than one billion Catholics around the world. Great events such as the *Giubileo* in 2000 or the ceremonial funeral of Pope John Paul II and the installation of his successor Benedict XVI in 2005 drew hundreds of thousands of believers and many onlookers.

museum covering some 3,000 sq m (32,291 sq feet), where the most important finds are displayed. Construction work on the long-awaited line C started in March 2007, and is scheduled for completion in the year 2011. The state-of-the-art line will be some 34.5 km (21.4 miles) long and will have 30 stations, from the east of the city to the north. Trains will be computer-controlled and driverless.

THE HIGHLIGHTS

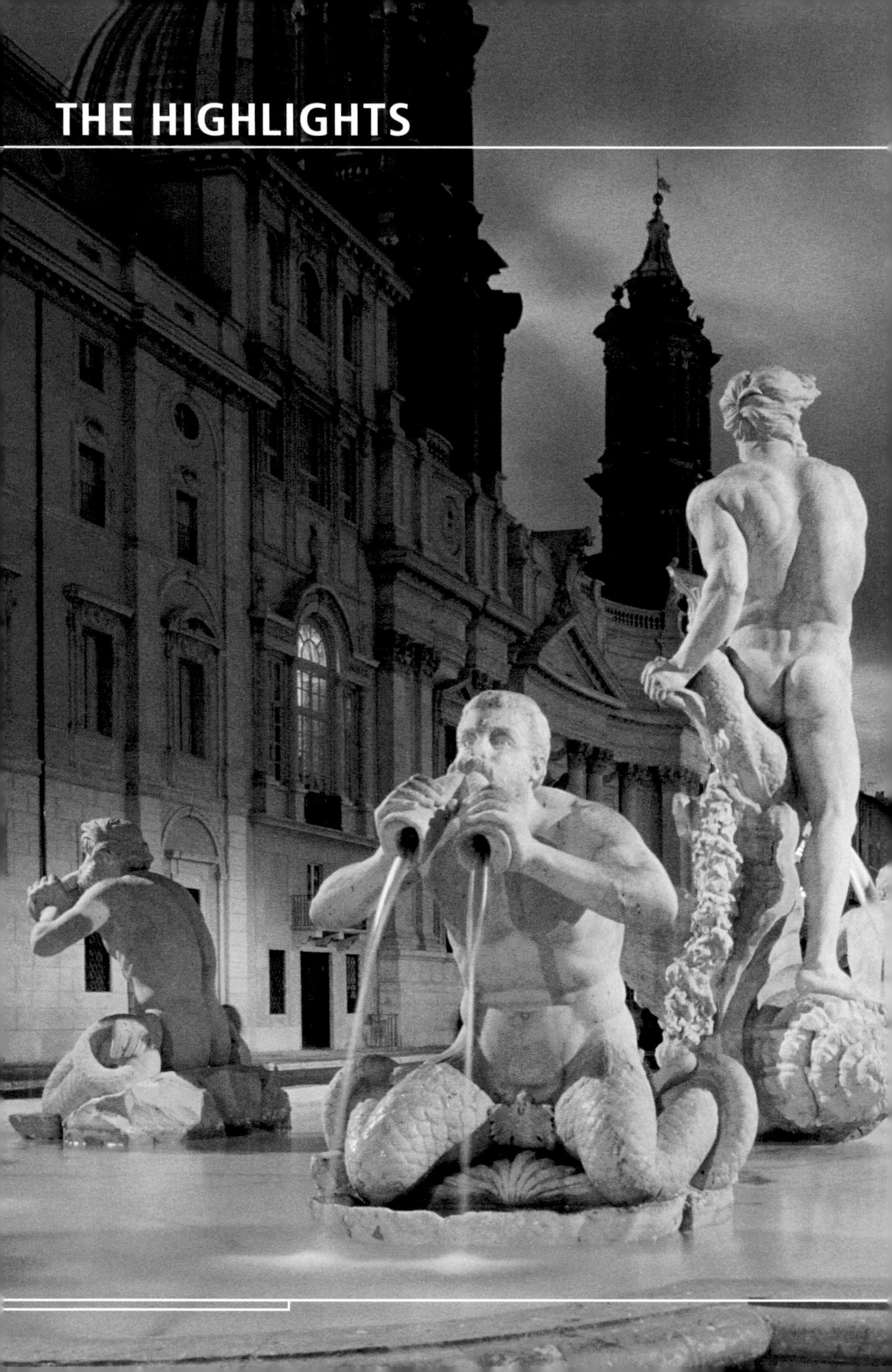

CENTRO STORICO

Rome's origins are shrouded in mystery and legend – archeological evidence appears to support the belief that it was founded on the Palatine Hill, one of the seven hills of Rome. The city, now home to millions, was highly populated and important even in ancient times, and was one of the founding cities of Western civilization. The hills were first settled in the Iron Age, spreading out to the valleys, and over the course of the centuries the "knee", the bend in the River Tiber, was also settled with increasing numbers. Inevitably, as the number of people multiplied, so did the buildings. Today the historic area around the Piazza del Popolo, the Spanish Steps, the Piazza Venezia, and the bend in the Tiber forms the heart of the Eternal City.

1. Piazza del Popolo
2. Ara Pacis Augustae
3. Piazza di Spagna
4. Piazza della Rotonda
5. San Luigi dei Francesi
6. Piazza Navona
7. Campo de´ Fiori
8. Memorial to Victor Emmanuel II

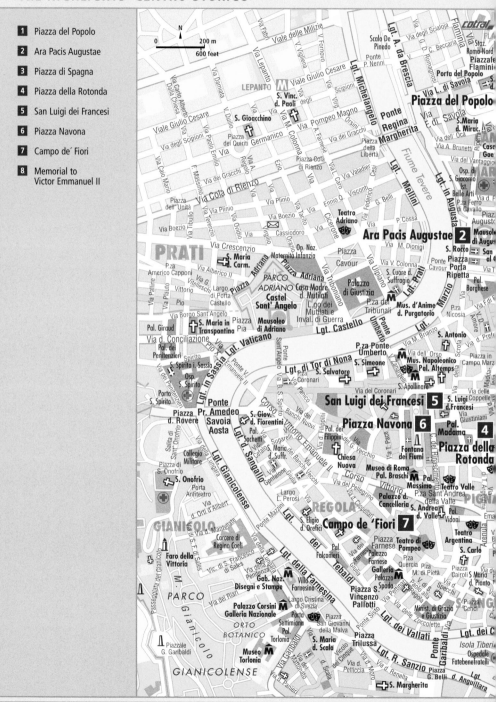

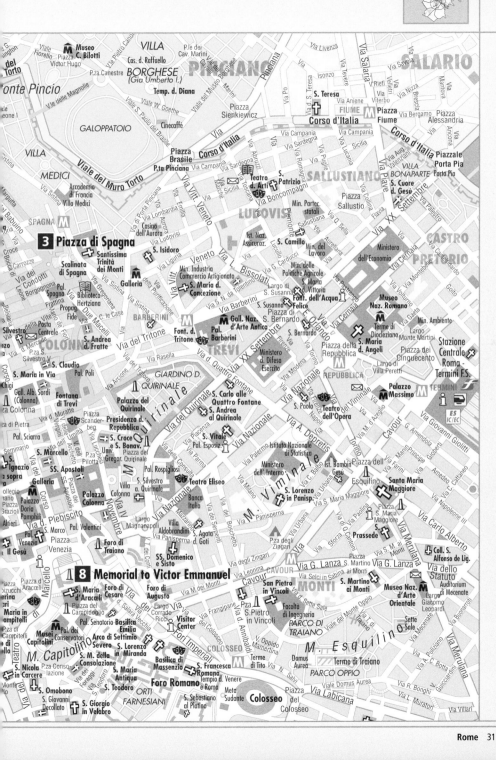

THE HIGHLIGHTS:
CENTRO STORICO

In the middle of the square is an ancient Egyptian obelisk, brought to Rome by Augustus (large image); at the entrance to the Via del Corso are the twin baroque churches of Santa Maria in Montesanto and Santa Maria dei Miracoli (small images, below and right). Public executions used to take place in the square, but ended in the early 19th century.

TIP Rosati

A beautifully positioned, elegant, and fashionable café. Good snacks, cakes, and drinks, but the prime location has its price.

Piazza del Popolo 5a;
Tel 06 322 58 59; 7.30–24.00,
daily; Metro A Flaminio.

PIAZZA DEL POPOLO **1**

People approaching the city from the north in days gone by would have entered through a gate in the Aurelian Walls, the Porta del Popolo, arriving at the Piazza del Popolo. The "square of the people" we see today is the work of the architect Giuseppe Valadier, who wanted to "open up" Rome. When he started to redesign the piazza in 1816, he left the 1,500-year-old *porta* standing, as well as the 17th-century twin churches, Santa Maria in Montesanto and Santa Maria dei Miracoli, which flank the entrance to the Via del Corso to the south. On either side of the churches, the Via del Babuino and the Via di Ripetta lead out at an oblique angle into the very heart of the old city; the layout is known as *il Tridente* because the three streets diverge like the prongs of a trident, an ancient weapon used in gladiatorial combat. To the east of the square, steps lead to the Pincio Hill.

The Altar of Peace (large image) is decorated with superb reliefs finely carved from Carrara marble. With the theme of civil peace, they depict the emperor and his family in acts of piety. Next to the entrance doors, there are allegorical scenes, and on the walls to the north and south a procession of members of the emperor's family is shown (right).

TIP Buccone

Lovers of good wine from every region of Italy are in good hands in this shop, located in a 17th-century building.

Via di Ripetta 19–20;
Tel 06 361 21 54; 10.00–1.00;
Bus 117, 119.

ARA PACIS AUGUSTAE 2

The Via di Ripetta leads from the Piazza del Popolo to the Tiber. Today, it is the site of two historic memorials to Augustus, Rome's first emperor: the Ara Pacis, which is dedicated to him, and the mausoleum designed by him. The Ara Pacis, or Altar of Peace, was commissioned by the Senate in 9 BC to celebrate the triumphal return of Augustus and the end of the civil war; it was originally located on the Campus Martius. Over the centuries, parts of the monument became scattered about Italy in various museums and it had to be reconstructed; it was opened to the public in its current location in 1938. The altar has been protected by a glass covering since 2006. The mausoleum is stylistically based on Etruscan barrow graves. Built of stone and cylindrical in shape, it housed burial chambers for the emperor and his family. It was topped with earth, planted with cypresses, and crowned with a bronze statue of the dead.

THE HIGHLIGHTS: CENTRO STORICO

TIP The Hassler Rooftop Restaurant

Officially the Spanish Steps (image, below right) are named the Scalinata della Trinità dei Monti, after the French church at the top. At the foot of the steps, Bernini's Fontana della Barcaccia, represents a half-sunken boat (image, below left). Right: Opened in 1760, the illustrious clients of the Caffè Greco are said to include Keats and Casanova.

Directly next to the church of Santa Trinità dei Monti, the roof terrace restaurant of the Hotel Hassler provides a fantastic view and excellent cuisine.

Piazza Trinità dei Monti 6; Tel 06 69 93 40; 12.30–14.30 and 19.30–22.30, daily; Metro A Spagna.

On the Via del Babuino, the left tine of *il Tridente*, lies the Piazza di Spagna – so called because in the 17th century the Spanish ambassador had his residence here. For young Romans, this area used to be dangerous at night. People would disappear without trace – forced into service in the Spanish army. The fountain in the square, La Fontana della Barcaccia, is said to have been commissioned by Pope Urban VIII. The popular name of the Spanish Steps, built between 1723 and 1726 by Francesco de Sanctis, is misleading: the steps connect the square with the French church of Santa Trinità dei Monti, and it was a French cardinal who suggested their construction, as a tribute to the king of France. However, the cardinal's idea was not without opposition and initially several popes refused to allow the steps to be built. The nearby Caffè Greco has been popular with booklovers for almost 250 years.

From A for Armani to Z for Zegna – every Roman child knows the alphabet of the fashion houses. When Count Giorgini staged a fashion show for an international audience in Florence, it was the start of the modern world's love affair with Italian design and taste. Italian fashion is one of the country's chief exports, but inevitably high quality comes at a price.

SHOPPING – HIGH FASHION, AND MORE

The area around Piazza di Spagna – the Via dei Condotti, the Via Borgognona, and part of the Via del Babuino – is a mecca for lovers of high fashion. This is where you will find all the great names in haute couture such as Versace, Gucci, Prada, Armani, Valentino, and Laura Biagiotti. In 2007, Fendi opened a store on the Via Borgognona in a 15th-century villa, where her creations are displayed like works of art. The showpiece is a 9-m (29-foot) long chandelier made from precious Murano glass. The luxury jeweler Bulgari has a branch at the entrance to the Via dei Condotti, also selling handbags and other accessories. If you are interested in antiques, make sure you take a stroll down the Via del Babuino. The Via del Corso caters for fashion with a younger feel. The music shop Ricordi has a "mediastore" on this street. Also on the Via del Corso, in the Piazza Colonna, there is a branch of the upmarket department store chain Rinascente.

Not quite as exclusive, but well worth a visit, are the shops on the Via Nazionale, the Via del Tritone, and the Via Cola di Rienzo (on the other side of the river, north of Castel Sant'Angelo).

For more clothes shopping try the Via del Governo Vecchio, where you can buy everything from jewelry and accessories to tailored coats and bathing suits. The prices are not the cheapest in Rome, but the charming, bustling Via del Governo Vecchio is very picturesque.

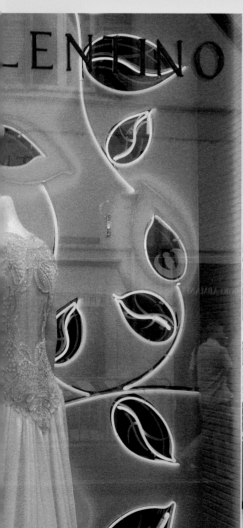

The Romans called the circular Pantheon the Rotunda. Today, the square that takes its name, the Piazza della Rotonda, is a hive of activity (large images, below). It was constructed under Clement XI, when several buildings on the site were pulled down. Right: The 9-m (29-foot) wide opening in the "vault of heaven" is the ancient Pantheon's sole source of light.

INFO Pantheon

With its imposing dome, the Pantheon is one of the most fascinating buildings of ancient Rome; within are the tombs of King Victor Emmanuel II and of Raphael.

Piazza della Rotonda; Tel 06 68 30 02 30; Mon–Sat 8.00–19.30, Sun 9.00–18.00, public holidays 9.00–13.00; Bus 116.

West of the Via del Corso, on the Piazza della Rotonda, is one of the most impressive buildings of ancient times: as its Greek name implies, the Pantheon was a temple dedicated to all the gods. This domed structure has had a varied history: first built in 27 BC, it was destroyed by fire in AD 80 and reconstructed during the reign of Emperor Hadrian (117–138). The round opening in the dome, the *oculus* (eye), had a mystical significance, creating a link to the world of the gods. In the 5th century, the building was closed, but subsequently converted into a Christian church by Pope Boniface IV, who, in so doing ensured its preservation. Used as a mausoleum from the time of the Renaissance, the tombs of Raphael and Annibale Carracci can be found inside, and also those of King Umberto I and Victor Emmanuel II, the first king of a unified Italy, though it has been a republic since 1946.

The frescoes created by Raphael and his pupils in 1518 for the Villa Farnesina in the district of Travestere portray the myth of Cupid and Psyche – including the *Council of the Gods* (large image). Right: Guido Reni's fresco (1612–14) in the central hall of the Casino Rospigliosi-Pallavicini in Rome shows Apollo pursuing Aurora, the goddess of the dawn, in his chariot.

THE ROMAN GODS

The ancient Romans recognized many deities and also adopted foreign gods, such as the Egyptian goddess Isis. As their empire expanded, the Romans would grant equal status to the gods of the conquered lands as to their own deities and built sanctuaries for the new gods in Rome. Hence the cult of Mithras, usually depicted as a young man, arrived in Rome from Persia and was taken to parts of Germany and Britain as the Romans made their way across Europe. Up until the 5th century BC, the Roman gods were personifications of nature; then, under the influence of the Etruscans, they also accepted but renamed the Greek pantheon. Father of the Greek gods Zeus became Jupiter, and his wife Hera became Juno. The ten other chief Roman gods were: Apollo (poetry), Ceres (fertility), Diana (the hunt), Mars (war), Minerva (wisdom), Venus (love), Neptune (the sea), Vesta (the hearth and its fire) and Vulcan (fire and metal working); Mercury was the messenger of the gods, as well as the god of thieves and merchants. Other gods were added to the 12 main ones, including Bacchus, the god of wine, and Pluto, the lord of the underworld. Officially, they all stopped existing in Christian times; their temples were closed or, like the Pantheon, were converted into churches. However, the old gods lived on in art and literature, and they continue to enrich our lives to this day.

THE HIGHLIGHTS: CENTRO STORICO

The series of three paintings produced by Caravaggio between 1597 and 1602 for the Contarelli chapel in the church of San Luigi dei Francesi is its most famous work (images, below and right). The paintings show scenes from the life of Matthew the evangelist – *The Calling of St Matthew, The Inspiration of St Matthew*, and *The Martyrdom of St Matthew*.

TIP Gelateria Giolitti

This famous ice-cream shop was established more than 100 years ago; naturally, it believes that it sells the best ice-cream in Italy. Choose from over 60 flavours, in an interior with a nostalgic feel.
Via Uffici del Vicario 40; Tel 06 699 12 43; 7.00–2.00, daily; Bus 62, 63.

This church, dedicated to French king Louis IX who was canonized in 1297, is a place of worship for French residents in Rome – the coat of arms on the gable features lilies, the emblem of France. On the façade are figures from French history including Charlemagne, St Jeanne de Valois, and St Clotilde. Construction began in 1518 and after a lengthy interruption was completed in 1589, with the aid of financial contributions from the French king. The church has an opulent interior, with three naves. A side chapel contains three large paintings by Caravaggio (1571–1610), showing scenes from the life of the apostle Matthew: his calling, his meeting with the angel, and his martyrdom. Caravaggio is considered the first of the great baroque painters and a master in the use of dramatic lighting; he is well known for his *chiaroscuro* ("light-dark") painting and strong realism, as well as for the religious subjects of most of his works.

THE HIGHLIGHTS:
CENTRO STORICO

TIP Tre Scalini

To finance the Fountain of the Four Rivers, special taxes were raised in 1651, including a tax on bread – which was not a popular move. Gianlorenzo Bernini's allegory of the Ganges on the Fountain of the Four Rivers (image, below left); the Fountain of Neptune (image, below right). Right: Local artists display their work in the Piazza Navona.

The Piazza Navona is a much-loved meeting place by day and night. This popular ice-cream shop is an ideal place for a break and a delicious *gelato* or a fruity *granita*. Try the *Tartufo*!
Piazza Navona 28; Tel 06 68 80 19 96; Thurs–Tues 9.00–22.00; Bus 70, 81.

This piazza grew into its present form over several centuries. Its elongated shape indicates that it was once a stadium, built by Caesar and expanded in the year 85 under Domitian. In the early Middle Ages, a church was built on the site where St Agnes had suffered a martyr's death; living quarters and shops were constructed under the former spectator stands, which gradually developed into larger buildings. In 1477, Sixtus IV granted permission for a market to be opened here and horse races were held in the square until 1495, when it was paved. In the 17th and 18th centuries, the piazza was flooded and turned into a lake during the celebrations held by the powerful Pamphili family. In the mid-17th century, two rival architects were commissioned to improve the square: Gianlorenzo Bernini created the Fountain of the Four Rivers, and Francesco Borromini rebuilt the church of Sant'Agnese in Agone.

In the unofficial ranking of the best Roman fountains, the most famous is the Fontana di Trevi (large image) – throw a coin in over your shoulder and it is said you will return to Rome one day; closely following are the fountains on the Spanish Steps and in the Piazza della Rotonda (small images below, from top). Right: Many of the fountains are decorated with wonderful sculptures and mosaics.

THE ROMAN FOUNTAINS

In Rome there is a fountain on almost every street corner and in almost every square – there are several hundred of them. The simplest kind consists of a bent metal outflow pipe, generally with a small basin beneath it. Passers-by can stop to quench their thirst at these nose-shaped pipes, which the Romans have affectionately nicknamed *nasoni* (big noses).

The large, elaborate, and artistically significant fountains are an indirect legacy of ancient times. They originated in the fountains that grew up at the sites of ancient shrines once dedicated to water spirits (*nymphaea*), at the ends of the aqueducts that transported drinking water into the city from the mountains. Three of these aqueducts are still intact and continue to supply several fountains: the Aqua Virgo supplies the Trevi Fountain; the Aqua Claudia supplies the Moses Fountain; and the Aqua Augusta ends in the waterfalls by the Villa Aldobrandini in Frascati. Apart from the Trevi, Rome's best-known fountain, built 1732–1762 by Salvi and Pannini, others to look out for include the Fontanella delle Tiare (Fountain of the Tiaras, 1927) in the Borgo district; the Fontanella del Facchino (The Porter, 1590) in the wall of Banco di Roma on Via Lata; the Fontana di Porta Cavalleggeri (1565) in the wall near the Vatican on Largo di Porta Cavalleggeri – whose basin is an ancient sarcophagus; Fontana dei Cavalli Marini (Seahorses) (1791) at the Villa Borghese.

THE HIGHLIGHTS: CENTRO STORICO

The lively market in the Campo de' Fiori still retains the bustling air of the medieval inns that once flourished here. In the middle of the piazza stands the hooded figure of Giordano Bruno (right), who was burned at the stake as a heretic, and now watches over the the piazza; it is no coincidence that he is looking towards the Vatican.

TIP Ar Galletto

If you can get a seat outside this simple but good *trattoria*, you'll have a wonderful view of the fountain and the Palazzo Farnese. Tasty Roman cuisine.

Piazza Farnese 102; Tel 06 686 17 14; Mon–Sat 12.15–15.15 and 19.15–23.00; Bus 116.

The Campo de' Fiori is a rectangular piazza which was once used for horse racing and executions – there was a permanent gibbet on the spot. The best-known offender put to death here was philosopher Giordano Bruno, who died at the stake on 17 February 1600. He was accused of heresy as, among other things, he was a proponent of heliocentrism, publicly doubting that the earth was the focal point of the universe. A memorial to him was erected in 1884, a gift of the Freemasons in a sign of protest against the Church: Pope Leo XII had accused the members of this secret order of being "destroyers of the faith".

Today the piazza is no longer used for sinister purposes. At odds with its dark past, its name means "field of flowers", harking back to the time when the area was just a meadow. During the day, flowers and local food are sold, and at night the square becomes a popular meeting place for young Romans.

Foreigners are expressly warned against taking a car onto the streets of the eternally jammed city. Cycling would be foolhardy and even by moped, despite being able to wind your way through the columns of cars and park easily, it's rarely a pleasure – there are simply too many cars and too little space and the driving style is simply too unpredictable for foreigners.

GETTING AROUND IN ROME

In order to protect both people and monuments from exhaust fumes, the Centro Storico has been declared a "blue zone", banned to private traffic. However, many Romans seem to know someone whose brother, sister, uncle, or aunt works for the authorities – and over 40,000 exceptions have been granted. As an outsider, driving a car in Rome is a risky business. Romans, like Italians in general, are good at communicating with their hands, even when driving, so foreign drivers in Rome not only need to know Italian road signs and traffic laws – a red traffic light is not necessarily a command to stop – they also need to be able to decipher even the most casual hand signals. Watch out for flashing headlights, which, rather than "after you" often mean "after me", while the horn is used extravagantly by all drivers to warn others of their presence. After midnight, though there may not be noticeably less traffic, Roman traffic lights are set to flash amber, indicating that any vehicle may proceed if the way is clear. Visitors should proceed with extreme caution and are advised to explore on foot or use public transport. There are only two lines on the underground rail system, the Metropolitana, but there are numerous taxis: licensed taxis are white or yellow and have a number; avoid the unlicensed ones. If you really want to venture out onto the roads, you can rent a scooter, but even this is not recommended for non-Romans.

THE HIGHLIGHTS: CENTRO STORICO

INFO Museo del Palazzo Venezia

The dazzling white limestone monument (images, below and right) on the Piazza Venezia has attracted its share of flack over the years, being given derogatory names by the locals, such as "the typewriter" or "the wedding cake". It took 26 years to build, and was officially opened in 1911. In the eastern section is the Museo Centrale de Risorgimento.

This Renaissance *palazzo* was used at times as a papal residence, and Mussolini also lived here. The museum has a first-class collection of Renaissance paintings and holds temporary exhibitions.
Via del Plebiscito 118; Tel 06 69 99 43 19; Tues–Sun 8.30–19.30; tourist bus 110.

MEMORIAL TO VICTOR EMMANUEL II

If someone shouted the slogan "*Viva Verdi!*" in the mid-19th century in Italy, he or she was not cheering the well-known opera composer but Victor Emmanuel II, who had ruled the kingdom of Piedmont-Sardinia since 1849. Many Italians wanted him to be the king (*re*) of a united Italy. The name "Verdi" was made up of the initial letters of the title that the monarch would be granted on ascending the throne: Vittorio Emanuele Re d'Italia. In 1861, the supporters of a united Italy finally had their wish and Victor Emmanuel became king of Italy. Born in 1820, he had taken part in the First Italian War of Independence with his father, Charles Albert of Sardinia, and had also been the joint leader of the Risorgimento (the movement for unification) with the freedom fighter Garibaldi. The king was much loved by his people – though this love did not necessarily extend to his memorial, designed by Giuseppe Sacconi.

THE HIGHLIGHTS

ANCIENT ROME

The 20th-century Roman writer Alberto Moravia described Rome as a city that has more monuments than houses. As early as late antiquity, people were concerned about protecting this unique legacy. In 458, the Western Roman Emperor Majorian ordered that "everything that contributes to the brilliance of the city should be maintained in good order by the zeal of the citizens". With its many splendid churches and monuments such as the Colosseum, Rome's antiquities are its greatest attraction, drawing millions every year. Many first-time visitors are astounded by the wealth of ancient remains, understandably believing they have stepped into an open-air museum.

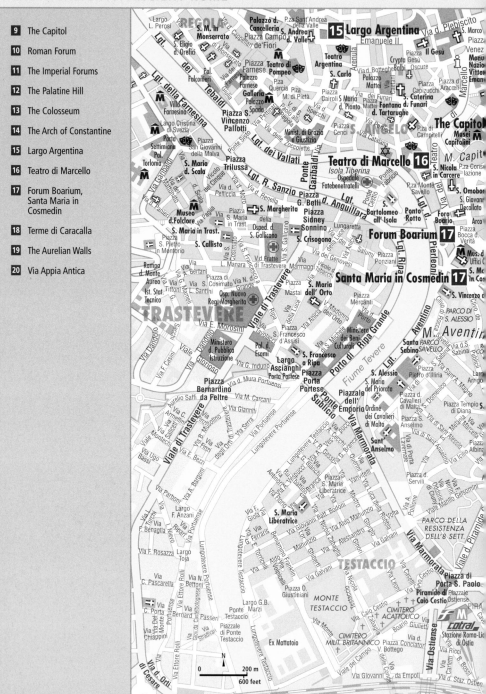

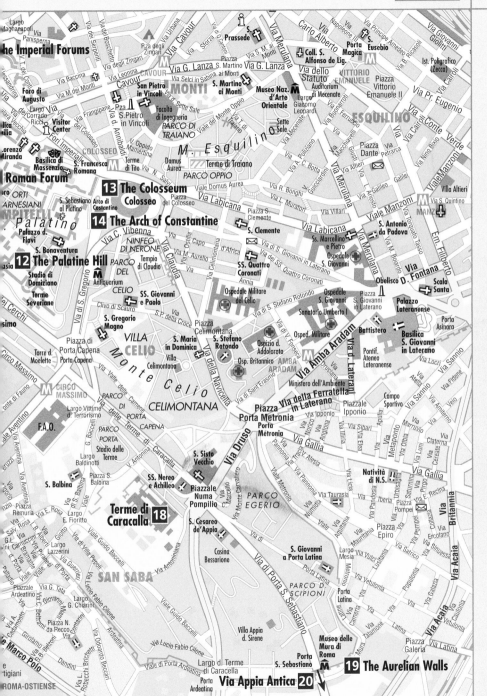

A copy of the equestrian statue of the stoic philosopher and emperor Marcus Aurelius – one of the so-called "Five Good Emperors" (small image, below left). The original is now in the Capitoline Museums. Michelangelo's Piazza del Campidoglio on the Capitol, once the heart of the Roman world (large image).

TIP Caffè Capitolino

Combine a visit to the Capitoline Museums with a short break in this *caffè*. You can enjoy a great view along with your espresso.

Piazza del Campidoglio 1;
Tel 06 67 10 24 75; Tues–Sun
9.00–19.30; Bus 64, 84.

In ancient times, there was a temple dedicated to Jupiter, the most important of the gods, on the top of the Capitol, reached along a winding path from the Forum to the south-east. Today you climb to the top from the west, up a flight of steps designed by Michelangelo, alongside which runs an older staircase leading to the church of Santa Maria in Aracoeli. Once at the top – it is the lowest of the seven hills of Rome – the visitor is in the heart of a piazza with paving laid out in a geometric pattern, also the work of Michelangelo. In the middle is the equestrian statue of Marcus Aurelius, the only equestrian bronze to have survived since antiquity, which escaped being melted down in the medieval period because it was thought that the rider was Constantine I, the first Christian Roman emperor. The Palazzo Senatorio on the piazza is the seat of the mayor of Rome.

In 1734, Pope Clement XII transformed the Palazzo Nuovo, built in the previous century, into a museum. Among its ancient treasures are the remains of a colossal statue of Emperor Constantine I (large image), the famous bronze *Capitoline Wolf*, and the bronze *Spinario* (small images, right) and *The Dying Gaul* (small image, below right). One of the highlights of the collection is the wonderful *Esquiline Venus* from the 1st century BC (see p. 175)

THE CAPITOLINE MUSEUMS

Two of the buildings in the square on top of the Capitol – the Palazzo dei Conservatori and the Palazzo Nuovo – are home to the Capitoline Museums. The collection is based on a series of ancient sculptures donated by Pope Sixtus IV and opened to the public in 1471. The best-known exhibit is the *Capitoline Wolf*, a bronze statue of the famous wolf who, according to legend, suckled the twins Romulus and Remus. The two human figures – sometimes ascribed to Antonio Pollaiuolo, sometimes to Gianlorenzo Bernini – are a later addition. The wolf herself was thought to be an Etruscan work from the 5th century BC, but it appears that she might be younger than previously assumed. During restoration work, it was found that the casting technique used was unknown to the Etruscans. It is now thought that this sculpture might have been produced some time in the Middle Ages. Another famous piece is the *Spinario*, a statue of a boy removing a thorn from his foot, a recurrent theme in ancient sculpture. The Capitoline's Pinacoteca (picture gallery) mostly contains works from the 16th and 17th centuries. Notable canvases are *The Holy Family*, by Dosso Dossi; *Head of a Boy* by Lodovico Carracci; the fine *Double Portrait of Brothers Lucas and Cornelis de Wael*, by Van Dyck. The remains of a giant statue of Emperor Constantine (the head, a foot, hands...) are on display in the gallery's entrance courtyard.

THE HIGHLIGHTS:
ANCIENT ROME

The Roman Forum was the heart of ancient Rome (images, below and right). Today these ruins show how the Romans used their urban spaces and are evidence of the secular power of the past: the triumphal arch of Septimius Severus is flanked by the Temple of Saturn and the Temple of Vespasian, with a backdrop of the baroque Santi Lucae Martina church.

INFO Roman Forum

Very informative guided tours can be booked through Romamirabilia (info@romamirabilia.com).

Entrances: Arco di Settimio Severo, Largo Romolo e Remo, Arco di Tito, and from the Via di San Teodoro; Tel 06 699 01 10; 9.00 to 1 hour before sunset, daily; Metro B Colosseo.

"Now I'll show you the place in the city where / Any person is most easily found, / So that you do not have to spend much time running about when you / Want to meet him, whether he's a rogue, or whether he's an honest man", wrote the poet Plautus (250–184 BC). He was speaking of the Roman Forum (Forum Romanum) – the complex of squares and buildings (erected from the 6th century BC onward) situated between the Palatine Hill and the Capitol. It was here that religious ceremonies and political meetings took place, speeches were made, and goods were sold. The Roman Forum was full of people daily – discussing business, meeting friends, or just whiling away the hours. The building complex included the Regia, a royal residence, and the House of the Vestal Virgins. When the Roman Empire fell, the Forum buildings fell into decay. In the Middle Ages, the square was known as Campo Vaccino, the cow pasture.

THE HIGHLIGHTS: ANCIENT ROME

Located between Trajan's Forum and the lower slopes of the Quirinal Hill, Trajan's markets were the precursor of the modern shopping mall (large image). Built in the early 2nd century, the market had around 150 shops selling wine, oil, and food on the lower level and offices on the upper level. Right: Relief on Trajan's Column, made from 17 blocks of marble.

TIP Cavour 313

Cozy, wood-lined *enoteca* close to the Forum, with simple dishes and a very good and extensive wine list.

Via Cavour 313; Tel 06 678 54 96; Mon–Sat 12.30–14.30 and 19.30–0.30, Sun 19.30–0.30; Bus 75, 84.

By the end of the republican era, and in spite of the various civil wars that had taken place over 60 or so years, the population of Rome had grown so much that the Forum, then about 500 years old, was no longer large enough. Caesar carried out an initial expansion in 54 BC, financing the work using booty recovered from the war against the Gauls. Around 50 years later, when the population was approaching one million, Emperor Augustus carried out a second expansion of the area. In AD 97, under Emperor Nerva, the square in front of a temple to Minerva was added. A final phase of expansion took place under Emperor Trajan, who ruled between 98 and 117. A 38-m (124-foot) high column was erected in the forum named after him; it is decorated with a long spiral relief celebrating his two victorious military campaigns against the Dacians, though most of the carving depicts the Roman army in action.

THE HIGHLIGHTS: ANCIENT ROME

INFO The Palatine Hill

Large image, below left: Fresco in the Domus Augustana, the lavish palace built by Emperor Domitian (around 30 BC), and painted terracotta reliefs from the Temple of Apollo (large image, below right), around 36 BC – on the Palatine Hill. Right: The Farnese pavilions overlooking the Forum were built in the 16th century for a large private garden on the Palatine.

The Palatine is dotted with the ruins of ancient palaces and gardens with splendid views over the Forum. The entry charge is high, but includes admission to the Colosseum.

Entrances: Via di San Gregorio or the Arch of Titus (Via Sacra); Tel 06 39 96 77 00; 9.00 to 1 hour before sunset; daily; Metro B Colosseo.

The Palatine Hill, the legendary site of the foundation of the city, bears the oldest traces of human settlement in Rome, dating back to the 10th century BC. Of the seven classic hills of the city, it became the place of choice for the rich and famous of ancient times on which to build their lavish residences. The statesman and great orator Cicero settled here, as did the poet Catullus. The Palatine Hill was also the home of Emperor Augustus and his wife Livia. Later emperors, such as Tiberius, Caligula, and Domitian also enjoyed living out their supremely luxurious lifestyles in magnificent palaces on the hill, but many have not survived. Domitian built the Domus Flavia for state purposes and the Domus Augustana as a private palace. The remains of the former residence of the emperor Tiberius are now covered by the Farnese Gardens, which were laid out in the 16th century.

THE HIGHLIGHTS:
ANCIENT ROME

TIP Nerone

The *velarium* was a giant retractable awning made of canvas that could be extended to cover two-thirds of the arena, to protect the spectators from the sun or, less frequently, the rain. The emperor, city administrators, and vestal virgins sat on a podium reserved for them, while the senators had to make do with rows of ivory armchairs.

Just a few minutes on foot from the Colosseum, Nerone offers simple *trattoria*-style meals at reasonable prices.

Via delle Terme di Tito 96; Tel 06 481 79 52; Mon–Sat 12.00–15.00 and 19.00–23.00; Metro B Colosseo.

Emperor Nero's palace once stood on the site of this vast ancient arena. It was one of the many wooden buildings destroyed in the Great Fire of Rome in 64 BC, which famously occurred during Nero's reign. In around 72, his successor Vespasian commissioned the three-floor stone arena, the remains of which visitors now see today. Construction was partially financed by the gold and treasure that fell into the hands of the Romans when they plundered the temple at Jerusalem. When finished, the building was capable of seating between 50,000 and 70,000 spectators. The games held to mark the official opening of the Colosseum lasted 100 days, during which thousands of animals were killed for the amusement of the baying crowds. The poet Martial (40–102) paid tribute to the emperor Vespasian with the following lines: "Rome has returned to its people, and under your government, Emperor, people are being entertained".

THE HIGHLIGHTS: ANCIENT ROME

TIP Pasqualino

Although Constantine attributed his victory over Emperor Maxentius to a vision of Christ, his triumphal arch (large image) does not display any Christian iconography. Instead, reliefs and statues were plundered from older memorials from the times of Trajan, Hadrian, and Marcus Aurelius (right).

There are few restaurants around the Colosseum that do not cater solely for tourists. But close by, this *trattoria* provides good food and even has a few Roman customers.

Via dei Santi Quattro 66; Tel 06 700 45 76; Tues–Sun 12.00–14.00 and 19.00–23.00; Metro B Colosseo.

The custom of erecting a triumphal arch for victorious commanders was introduced to Rome by the Etruscan kings. One of the greatest memorials of this type stands near the Colosseum: the Arch of Constantine was erected to the emperor Constantine I by the Senate in AD 315 – three years after the emperor's victory over his rivals. It was Constantine who was the first to give full recognition to Christianity as a religion. Some of the structural elements were taken from memorials originally dedicated to former Roman rulers: the statues of four prisoners on the north side of the arch, for example, came from a memorial to Emperor Trajan; the reliefs below were taken from a memorial to Marcus Aurelius. Reliefs inside the arch tell of Trajan's victory over the Dacians. The arch spans the Via Triumphalis, the route taken by victorious military commanders awarded a triumph by the city, a public celebration of their achievements on the battlefield.

THE HIGHLIGHTS:
ANCIENT ROME

INFO Teatro Argentina – Teatro di Roma

It is not certain after whom or what the Largo di Torre Argentina square was named (images, below and right) – perhaps after Johannes Burkard, a papal master of ceremonies (*argentoratum* in Latin) who once lived nearby or after the silversmiths' shops in the area (*argentarii*).

Many operas have premiered at the Teatro Argentina, including some by the great Italian composers Rossini and Verdi. The Teatro Argentina regularly stages the great classics.
Largo Torre Argentina 56;
Tel 06 684 00 03 45;
performances Oct–June; Tram 8.
www.teatrodiroma.net

Four temples from the republican, pre-empire era are to be found in this former *area sacra* (holy area) as well as the remains of the "Teatro di Pompey". The oldest temple, dedicated to Feronia – revered as the protecting goddess of all freed slaves and the guardian of the springs in the city – is thought to have been constructed in around 300 BC. Another temple was probably built to celebrate the victory of Catulus over the Carthaginians in 241 BC. The square is part of the Campus Martius (The Field of Mars), an area of publicly owned land used as a place of public assembly and for military parades. Today the locals call the Largo the Cat's Forum, because large numbers of cats live around the ancient ruins. In 2001 the cat population in the old city was officially recognized as a "biocultural legacy" – *i gatti* enjoy special protection and are cared for here in the Largo Argentina by volunteers.

THE HIGHLIGHTS: ANCIENT ROME

Next to the Teatro di Marcello are three Corinthian columns and a section of a frieze (large image). They originally belonged to the Temple of Apollo, in which the Romans stored many of the works of art they stole from the Greeks in the 2nd century BC, prompting the vogue for all things Greek in Rome.

INFO Concerti al Tempietto

In the summer, music lovers can listen to classical music as part of the *Concerti al Tempietto*, open-air performances.

Area Archeologica del Teatro di Marcello, Via del Teatro di Marcello; Tel 06 67 10 38 19; July–Sept; Bus 44, 63, 81.

Several temples had to be demolished to make way for this theater on the ancient Campus Martius (Field of Mars). Planned by Julius Caesar, it was completed by Emperor Augustus, who named the building after his nephew, his designated successor, who had died young. The building could hold 15,000 spectators and for some events it could take as many as 20,000. Nevertheless, it was one of the smallest of its kind in Rome. It was used as a theater until around AD 400; after that time, its walls were plundered for stone for other buildings until the Savellis, one of the noblest families in the city, ordered its conversion into a fortress in the 13th century. Later, the two floors of arcades were shored up from the outside and apartments built on top; in the 16th century it became a giant palace for the Orsinis, another noble family. English architect Sir Christopher Wren took inspiration from the building for his design for the Sheldonian Theatre in Oxford.

According to legend, if a liar places a hand in the Bocca della Verità (Mouth of Truth), it will bite off their fingers (large image). Right: The church of Santa Maria in Cosmedin dates from the 6th century. In the 16th century, the last Roman Catholic archbishop of Canterbury, Cardinal Reginald Pole, was made a titular deacon of the church.

TIP Moschino

A typical Roman-style *osteria*, excellent cuisine, an ideal place to stop. The ham for the antipasto is sliced by hand; outstanding fettuccine and a piece of ricotta tart to finish.

Piazza Benedetto Brin 5;
Tel 06 513 94 73; daily except
Sun; Metro B Garbatella.

From the city's earliest days, there were many places in which the people could gather together in addition to the Forum Romanum but they were almost exclusively devoted to the sale of food and other goods, or domestic animals. The most important were the Forum Holitorium, the vegetable market, and the Forum Boarium, the cattle market. Both were located close to the ancient port on the Tiber, where there was also a temple (later converted into a Christian church) devoted to the Portunus, the patron saint of ports. The area that once made up the cattle market is today called the Piazza della Bocca della Verità – named after a stone mask of a Triton (god of the sea) dating from the 4th century BC, built into the portico of the church of Santa Maria in Cosmedin. The ancient stone is said to have been once used as a cover for a drainage channel – a rather disappointingly mundane use for the effigy of such a mighty god.

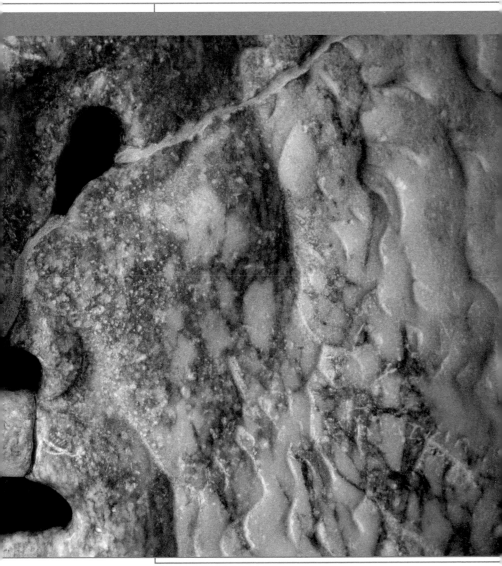

Professional fighters, the gladiators fought each other or wild animals, sometimes to the death, for the entertainment of the crowds. Though technically slaves – they were normally prisoners of war, criminals, or slaves – successful gladiators could buy their freedom after three years. Some men volunteered to fight as gladiators, drawn by the prospect of fame or money, as they were allowed to keep the money they won.

THE ROMAN ARENA

One of the first great pleasure palaces constructed for the people was the hippodrome the Circus Maximus dating from the 4th century BC. Light, two-wheeled chariots raced around the oval arena, pulled by two to seven horses. Fatal crashes were quite frequent, though on the whole it was far less gruesome entertainment than the so-called games held in the large amphitheaters. Built between AD 72 and 80, the largest of these, the Colosseum, was particularly famous. It could seat around 50,000 spectators – or as many as 70,000 according to some estimates. The seating was strictly regimented: the best seats, identified by name, were reserved for the senators, while women were seated right at the top in the worst seats. At the official opening of the Colosseum, 3,000 gladiators lost their lives, and countless animals were slaughtered – many were imported from the province of Africa for this purpose. Gladiators fought against each other in the arena, and if the emperor gave the infamous "thumbs down" sign, the loser was killed by the victor. The origin of gladiatorial combat is thought to lie in the battles fought by slaves forced to fight to the death at the funerals of distinguished aristocrats in the 3rd century BC. The combats gradually became divorced from the funeral ceremonies and were seen as a way for wealthy citizens to proclaim their influence and power.

THE HIGHLIGHTS: ANCIENT ROME

TIP Tramonti e Muffati

A marble bust of Emperor Caracalla (image, below left), who sought to win over the people by building the Caracalla Baths; mosaic floors and frescoes created a sophisticated atmosphere for bathers (images, below middle and right). There was even a public library in the complex. Right: A park was created on the site in around 1900.

A delicious selection of cheeses, a wide range of sausages, and a daily menu is on offer at this cozy *enoteca*, a short distance from the Via Appia.

Via di Santa Maria Ausiliatrice 105; Tel 06 780 13 42; evenings only, reservation recommended; Metro A Furio Camillo, Colli Albani.

The Romans had a well-developed bathing culture. As early as the 2nd century BC public bathing facilities were widely available. The Roman emperors knew that they could buy the goodwill of the people by constructing public facilities such as baths. Entry was free, and they were used both for personal hygiene and as places for sport and leisure. One of the great bathing complexes was the Caracalla Baths (Terme di Caracalla), which could cater for 1,600 at a time, and up to 6,000 people visited the extensive facilities daily. Inside the Terme di Caracalla were a *caldarium* (a room with hot, moist air), a *tepidarium* (a warm room), *frigidarium* (a cold room), covered walkways, a gymnasium for wrestling and boxing, a swimming pool, and other facilities. Heating was provided by a hypocaust, a system in which heat created by the burning of wood and coal was spread under the floor of the building, which was raised on pillars.

THE HIGHLIGHTS: ANCIENT ROME

INFO Museo delle Mura

Rome can thank the Aurelian Walls for its survival over the centuries (large image). They defined the boundary of the city and performed a significant defensive role until the 19th century. The Porta San Sebastiano leads out onto the Via Appia Antica (small image, below). Right: The Pyramid of Cestius stands on the road to Ostia.

This museum provides information about the history and construction of the Aurelian defensive walls in the 3rd century and offers the only public access to the walls.

Via di Porta San Sebastiano 18; Tel 06 70 47 52 84; Tues–Sat 9.00–14.00; Bus 118, 218.

After Rome was invaded by the Gauls in 370 BC, the Servian Walls were erected, the first defensive walls to be built around Rome. They were 11.5 km (7 miles) long and had 16 gates and were made from huge stone blocks. Construction of a new wall began in the time of Emperor Aurelian (270–275) and was completed under his successor Probus. From the dimensions of the Aurelian Walls, it is evident just how much larger and more powerful Rome had become since the city was attacked by the Gauls: the new walls were 18 km (11 miles) long, 17 m (55 feet) high and 4 m (13 feet) wide, and had no less than 381 towers. Parts of the walls are still standing today. An unusual structure was incorporated into the walls: the Pyramid of Cestius near the Porta San Paolo is the tomb of Caius Cestius Epulonius (died 12 BC) and is a reminder of the enthusiasm for Egypt at that time.

One of the most important roads in ancient Rome, the Appian Way, with its original paving stones lined with cypresses and pines, evokes images of ancient times when the Romans buried their dead here at night (images, below and right). During the slave revolt of 73 BC, 6,000 of Spartacus' defeated slave army were crucified along this road.

TIP Cecilia Metella

A walk along the Via Appia (approximately two hours) is thirsty work – be sure to take some water with you. This restaurant on the first section of the Via Appia offers a fortifying and welcome stop.
Via Appia Antica 129;
Tel 06 513 67 43;
daily except Mon; Bus 118.

The Via Appia, constructed in 312 BC, served as both a military and trading route. Extended many times over the centuries, it led across the Italian peninsula to Brindisi. In around 450 BC, it was forbidden to bury the dead in the city, so the inhabitants of Rome began to inter their loved ones beside the arterial roads, which is why the Via Appia is lined with numerous family and communal graves. Today, the official start of the Via Appia is no longer in the Roman Forum, but at the Porta San Sebastiano, the city gate in the Aurelian Walls. Approximately 3 km (2 miles) out from the city is an impos-ing circular stone building, some 20 m (65 feet) in diameter. It contains the tomb of Cecilia Metella, the wife of a patrician. Under the ground on either side of the Via Appia, a network of labyrinthine catacombs, the burial place of the early Christians, spread out beneath the fields.

THE VATICAN

The Via della Conciliazione, begun by Mussolini in 1937 and completed in 1950, connects St Peter's Square to the Castel Sant'-Angelo on the western bank of the Tiber River. The road not only provides a physical link between Rome and the Vatican City, it is also a symbol of the reconciliation (*conciliazione*) between the Church and state that was achieved through the Lateran Pact of 1929. After the unification of Italy in 1870, the popes had been obliged to relinquish their position as secular rulers; the Lateran Pact recognized the Vatican as an independent state, and the pope still bears the title "Sovereign of the State of the Vatican City".

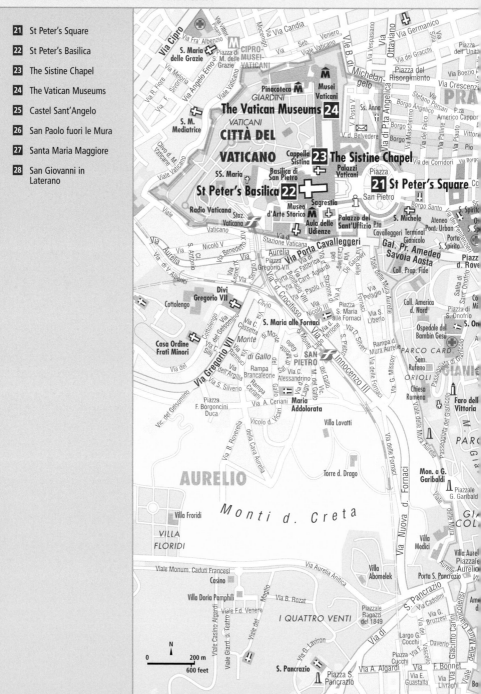

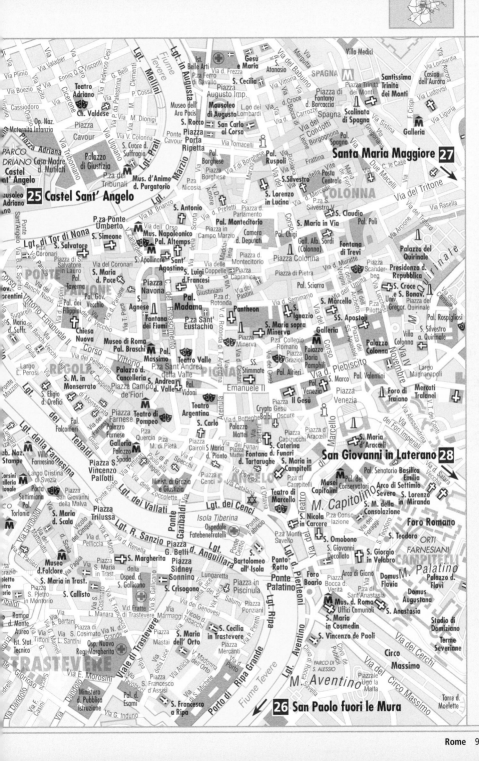

Right, from left: St Peter with Leo III and Charlemagne, as portrayed in the Middle Ages; the Holy Roman Emperor Henri IV (1050–1106), doing penance at Canossa; Boniface VIII (1235–1303) in the sacred college of cardinals. Important popes throughout history (large images): The first German pope for almost 500 years; Benedict XVI makes a papal address at Easter Mass in St Peter's Square. Small images below, from left: Martin V with King Sigismund at the Council of Constance in 1418; Pius IX; John XXIII; John Paul II.

THE PAPACY

The papacy has enjoyed a longer tradition than any other institution in the world. Uniting over one million Catholics in their faith, it is global in the best sense of the word. Its ceremonies and rituals are carried out with pomp and magnificence, which sets them apart from everyday life. Today, the papacy enjoys a good reputation, but this has not

always been the case. In his role as head of the Roman Catholic Church the pope is the focal point of the Catholic religion, therefore the reputation of the papacy and the Catholic Church is inextricably linked with the character of the man holding the office. Unfortunately not all popes in the past have been of pristine character. Renaissance popes, such as

Alexander VI (1492–1503), were notorious in their extravagance and lust for power, and some did not follow their own teaching, their real interest lying in the power of the highest office in the Catholic Church, rather than proclaiming the word of God. Yet among the fallible, there were also many good men, popes who were able to effect renewal and

reform, and so the history of the papacy is marked by highs and lows. As the first bishop of Rome, Peter was also the first to hold the title of pope. According to the words of Jesus taken from the Gospel and inscribed on the internal frieze of the great dome of St Peter's: "You are Peter, the Rock, and on this rock I will build my church" (Matthew 16,18).

THE HIGHLIGHTS: THE VATICAN

Monumental architecture: a view of St Peter's through the colonnades (large image). In the middle of the square is a 25-m (82-foot) Egyptian obelisk, brought to Rome from Heliopolis by Emperor Caligula in AD 37. Right: The dome of St Peter's Basilica, designed by Michelangelo, is a prominent feature of Rome's skyline.

INFO A papal audience

On Wednesday mornings you can take part in an audience with the pope. In summer this takes place in St Peter's Square, in winter in the Aula delle Udienze (Audience Hall).

For free tickets, apply to the Prefettura della Casa Pontificia; Tel 06 69 88 30 17; 09.00–13.00 and 17.00 –20.00, daily.

The square is at its most beautiful when the sun has set, the crowds of tourists have gone and the Roman night sky bathes the city in a magical light. Not actually square in shape, it was created at the height of the baroque period, after Luther's Protestant Reformation, when the Catholic Church wanted its sacred buildings to inspire awe in believers and reinforce its claim as the one true authority of God on earth. St Peter's Square was accordingly transformed into a breathtakingly beautiful forecourt to St Peter's Basilica. Designed by Bernini between 1656 and 1667, the square is 240 m (263 yards) wide, surrounded by colonnades of 284 columns topped by 140 statues of saints. To the left and right, at the two focal points of the giant oval, are two 14-m (46-foot) fountains. White marble stones are used as sundial markers, indicating the point where the tip of the obelisk's shadow lies at noon, as the sun enters each of the signs of the zodiac.

THE HIGHLIGHTS: THE VATICAN

INFO Climbing to the dome

By the end of the 15th century St Peter's was in a state of disrepair. Reconstruction began in 1506 and took around 150 years. Despite the number of architects involved, it retains a harmonious air (large image). Bernini's altar baldachin (small image, below). Right, from left: St Peter with the key; alabaster window depicting the Holy Spirit as a dove.

Climb the steep steps (or take an elevator part of the way) to the dome of St Peter's and you will be rewarded with a fantastic view over the Vatican and Rome.

Piazza San Pietro; 8.00–17.00, daily (as long as no mass is taking place); Metro A Ottaviano-San Pietro.

The present basilica, which has stood since the 16th century on the site of a former basilica built under Emperor Constantine, was for many years the largest Christian church in the world. The façade is some 45 m (147 feet) high and 115 m (377 feet) wide, and the height to the lantern crowning the dome is 132 m (433 feet). It bathes the interior in a gentle, mystical light. The gigantic interior of the cathedral can hold 60,000 worshippers. The most famous artists of their time worked on the design, including architects Bramante and Sangallo, painters Michelangelo and Raphael, and sculptors Bernini and Maderno. Near Bernini's tomb of Urban VIII you can descend to the grottoes, where the tomb of the basilica's namesake, Peter, is said to lie. In all there are some 100 tombs located within St Peter's, including over 90 popes, and James Francis Edward Stuart, the "Old Pretender", Catholic son of the deposed James II of England.

In his *Pietà* (1498–99), portraying the body of Christ cradled by his mother Mary after the Crucifixion, Michelangelo created one of the most important sculptures in St Peter's Basilica (large image). Right: His equally famous figure of Moses, made around 1515 for the tomb of Pope Julius II, is today located in the church of San Pietro in Vincoli. Small image, below right: a portrait of the artist by one of his pupils, painted around 1510.

MICHELANGELO

Along with Leonardo da Vinci, Michelangelo Buonarroti (1475–1564) is the most important artist of the Italian high Renaissance. Michelangelo learned fresco painting as a pupil of Domenico Ghirlandaio and looked to the old masters for inspiration, studying the sculptures of the ancient world. The creative focus for this brilliant painter, sculptor, and architect was the human figure. In order to achieve perfection in his representation of human anatomy, he is said not only to have drawn from life, but also to have secretly dissected corpses. In 1505 Pope Julius II summoned the artist to Rome to design a prestigious papal tomb, but when both this commission and his plans for a new St Peter's Basilica were rejected, Michelangelo returned, disenchanted, to Florence. However, a new challenge was to draw him back to Rome: the repainting of the ceiling of the Sistine Chapel. Michelangelo spent four years on this project, working virtually alone. High above ground balancing on a scaffolding, the work was also physically demanding. In 1547, he took over the supervision of the rebuilding of St Peter's: its dome being undoubtedly his greatest architectural achievement. Michelangelo's masterpieces as a sculptor include the *Pietà* in St Peter's and the figure of *David* in front of the Palazzo Vecchio in Florence (today, the original is in the Galleria dell'Accademia).

THE HIGHLIGHTS: THE VATICAN

INFO The Sistine Chapel

In contrast with its rich interior, the exterior of the Sistine Chapel is unadorned by architectural detail. Inside, the side walls show scenes from the lives of Christ and Moses. On the end wall is Michelangelo's altar fresco, *Last Judgement* (small image, below); his ceiling fresco (small image, right: *The Creation of Adam*) depicts the creation and the fall of man.

The papal chapel contains the world's most famous ceiling, with Michelangelo's depiction of the creation story. His altar fresco of the Last Judgement was painted later, between 1534 and 1541. The chapel is part of the Vatican Museums.
For opening times:
http://mv.vatican.va

The Sistine Chapel is where the cardinals hold papal conclaves, the ceremony in which a new pope is elected. Commissioned by Pope Sixtus IV in 1477, after whom it is named, it was originally not only a place of devotion but also a fortress, with walls 3 m (nearly 10 feet) thick. Sixtus had been at war with the republic of Florence, but by the time the chapel was completed, in 1480, the war was over and as a gesture of peace Lorenzo de' Medici, the ruler of Florence, sent some of his city's leading painters to Rome to decorate the interior of the chapel. The artists included Perugino, Botticelli, and Ghirlandaio. The walls were painted with scenes from the lives of Jesus and Moses, and the barrel-vaulted ceiling was transformed into a radiant blue sky with golden stars. Some 20 years later, Pope Julius II commissioned Michelangelo to repaint the ceiling, the work taking from 1508 to 1512.

THE HIGHLIGHTS:
THE VATICAN

Allow plenty of time to visit the Vatican Museums and their rich and varied collections dating from ancient and classical times, through the baroque to modern art. Large images below, from left: The *Laocoön* group from the 1st century; a bust of Caesar; *The Crucifixion of St Peter*, Guido Reni, 1604. Tickets can be bought in advance online.

TIP Dal Toscano

Close to the Vatican Museums, this restaurant has had some great reviews. It serves Tuscan delicacies such as *bistecca alla fiorentina*, the famous grilled steak.

Via Germanico 58–60;
Tel 06 39 72 57 17; Tues–Sun
12.30–15.00 and 20.00–23.15;
Metro A Ottaviano-San Pietro.

Many popes were avid collectors, while others commissioned works of art in the role of both patrons and clients. Today, the complex of Vatican Museums holds one of the largest collections of art in the world, ranging from ancient Egyptian and Etruscan objects to modern sacred art. The Pinacoteca (art gallery), opened by Pius XI in 1932, displays paintings from the 12th to the 19th centuries in a setting that befits their importance. The Missionary-Ethnological Museum brings together objects from around the world, from wherever the Catholic Church has been active. The Historical Museum has a collection of cars and carriages used by popes and cardinals, along with other objects and documents. In 2000, John Paul II officially opened the new entrance to the complex, featuring a huge spiral ramp reminiscent of New York's Guggenheim Museum. In his inaugural speech, John Paul II called the Vatican Museums "a bridge to the world" (see p. 166).

Raphael's frescoes in the Vatican include (right) *The School of Athens* (1510–11), which portrays the philosophers of ancient Greece; and (large image) *Fire in the Borgo* (1514), which shows Leo IV (pope 847–855) giving his blessing from the loggia, quenching the fire, and thus miraculously saving the church and its people. Small image, below right: Raphael's self-portrait from 1506.

RAPHAEL

Three geniuses left their mark on the Italian high Renaissance: Leonardo da Vinci, Michelangelo, and Raphael. Born in Urbino in 1483, Raphael's fame outshone that of any other painter for centuries, and no other artist was so widely imitated. The two quizzical and charming putti that Raphael added to his *Sistine Madonna* have been repro-duced on millions of greet-ings cards and souvenirs (the original is located in the Gemaldegalerie, Dresden, Germany).

Raphael's work was famous for its perfection and grace – the men and women in Raphael's paintings seem almost too beautiful to be true. He was accused by some of superficiality and sugary sweetness, which could be said of some of his religious paintings, but Raphael worked with the intensity and individuality of a true master, especially in regard to his portraits. He spent several years working in Florence, then moved to Rome in 1508, when, at the height of his creativity when he was inundated with commissions, Pope Julius II commissioned him to paint frescoes in a suite of rooms now known as the stanze. In 1514, he took over the management of the rebuilding of St Peter's Basilica, and in 1515 he was also given the responsibility of excavating and recording Roman antiquities. When he died of a fever in 1520, he was just 37 years of age, yet he had achieved fame and recognition throughout Europe.

THE HIGHLIGHTS:
THE VATICAN

TIP Tre Pupazzi

In 1667, Pope Clement IX commissioned Bernini, the master of the baroque, to create the white marble angels for the Ponte Sant'Angelo, the bridge across the Tiber on the approach to the Castel Sant'-Angelo (large image, below and small image, right). Each of the angels carries an instrument of the Passion of Christ (small images, below right).

This *taverna* in a building dating from the 17th century is just behind the Castel Sant'Angelo. If offers good Roman food, such as *fettuccine ai Tre Pupazzi*.
Borgo Pio 183;
Tel 06 686 83 71; Mon–Sat
12.00–14.30 and 19.00–23.00;
Metro A Ottaviano-San Pietro.

Emperor Hadrian (76–138) built the Castel Sant'Angelo as a mausoleum, but over the years it was gradually converted into a papal fortress. In the 13th century, a secret passage, the Passetto di Borgo, was constructed to connect the fortress with the papal palace. It was put to good use during the Sack of Rome in 1527, when Pope Clement VII and his cardinals escaped from the soldiers of Holy Roman Emperor Charles V. Almost the entire Swiss Guard was massacred in front of St Peter's, as they fought to buy time for the escaping pope. The Castel itself survived the attack – among its defenders were goldsmith and sculptor Benvenuto Cellini, who killed so many of the opposing troops that he later suffered pangs of remorse. However, as Cellini wrote, the pope "raised his hand and made the sign of the cross over my whole body, blessed me and forgave me all my murderous deeds that I had ever committed in the service of the Apostolic Church".

THE HIGHLIGHTS: THE VATICAN

The magnificent Venetian mosaics in the apse show Christ with Peter, Andrew, Luke, and Paul; the tomb of St Paul is said to lie beneath the altar (large image, below left). The stunning coffered ceiling (large image, below right); and the mosaics on the façade (small image, right). The central nave's 80 granite columns date from the 18th century.

TIP Trattoria Campagna

Hearty food, prepared wth seasonal ingredients, is a feature of the menu in this endearingly simple *trattoria*. Offal dishes feature alongside the pasta.

Via Ostiense 179; Tel 06 574 23 06; Mon–Sun (closed Sun evening); Metro B Garbatella.

As well as St Peter's, Rome has three other patriarchal basilicas, defined as churches that have a papal throne and an altar at which only the pope may read the mass: San Paolo fuori le Mura, Santa Maria Maggiore, and San Giovanni in Laterano. As its name indicates ("basilica outside the walls") San Paolo fuori le Mura lies to the south, beyond the city walls. It is dedicated to St Paul, who died a martyr's death in Rome, and who is said to be buried here. The vast basilica, founded in the 4th century, was almost completely destroyed by fire in July 1823, but has since been faithfully reconstructed using materials from several countries, including Egypt (alabaster pillars) and Russia (lapis lazuli and malachite). The main door is 20th century and incorporates part of the original door, which is 1,000 years old. The 13th-century cloisters, with brightly decorated, elaborately shaped columns, survived the fire.

Over the centuries, the basilica has been extended and modified, and today is a tapestry of artistic and architectural styles. The interior, with its three naves, reflects its original form (large image). The bell tower was added in the Middle Ages, and the coffered ceiling dates from the Renaissance (small image, right). The domes and façade are baroque in style.

TIP Agata e Romeo

A top-quality restaurant, specializing in variations on classic Italian dishes. The small, chilled *millefoglie* pastries have achieved legendary status.

Via Carlo Alberto 45;
Tel 06 446 61 15; Mon–Fri;
Metro A Vittorio Emanuele.

Legend has it that in 352 the Virgin Mary appeared to Pope Liberius in a dream, and commanded him to build a church in the place where he saw snow fall the next morning. As snow is a strange sight in Rome at any time of year, it is quite miraculous when it does occur – as in this case – on 5 August. When he awoke and saw the peak of the Esquiline Hill covered in a layer of white, Liberius lost no time in obeying the will of the Virgin. To commemorate the miracle responsible for the construction of the basilica, a service takes place every August in which white petals are scattered down on the worshippers. One of the four papal basilicas, it was used as a temporary papal residence when the Lateran Palace, the principal residence of the popes before they moved to the Vatican, fell into disrepair during the Avignon papacy. Despite being damaged in the earthquake of 1348, it retains the core of its original structure from the 5th century AD.

THE HIGHLIGHTS:
THE VATICAN

The basilica has seen many important events: in 1929, the Lateran Treaty regulating relations between the papacy and the Italian state was signed here, and on 2 April 2007, a mass took place during the case for beatification of Pope John Paul II. Below, right: The octagonal baptistery. Right: The Holy Staircase reputedly comes from Pontius Pilate's palace.

TIP Le Virtù in Tavola

Excellent fresh fish and meat, served with wines to match each dish. The cuisine is Sardinian, which is highly acclaimed by many Roman residents.

Via Domenico Fontana 26–28; Tel 06 77 20 63 63; Metro A San Giovanni.

The district in which this basilica lies is named after the once powerful Laterani family, who worked as administrators for the emperors. The family was disgraced at the start of the 4th century when one of them was accused of conspiring against Nero. Their land was confiscated, and subsequently fell into the hands of Emperor Constantine who had the first Christian basilica in Rome built on it. For Catholics, the Lateran basilica is the "mother of all churches", ranking even higher than St Peter's. It burned down twice, but was reconstructed in its original form on each occasion. Baroque architect Borromini altered parts of the interior in 1646 and in the 18th century the huge façade was superimposed. The church lies on the southern side of the Palazzo Lateranense, the papal residence until the start of the 14th century. The Scala Santa (Holy Staircase), opposite the palace, is a place of pilgrimage for many – pilgrims must climb it on their knees.

FURTHER AFIELD

Rome is a city of contrasts in many respects. Not only do old and new collide, but as you move from one part of the city to another it is as if you are entering a completely different world. A working-class district such as Testaccio is full of life and movement, while on the Aventine Hill it is so quiet you could almost forget that you are in a capital city. At the edge of the city are the Renaissance and baroque villas of noble families and senior clergymen. They are as famous for their extraordinary, lavish gardens as for the ornate architecture of the villas themselves. Further out, you can see the 20th-century official urban housing developments known as *borgate*.

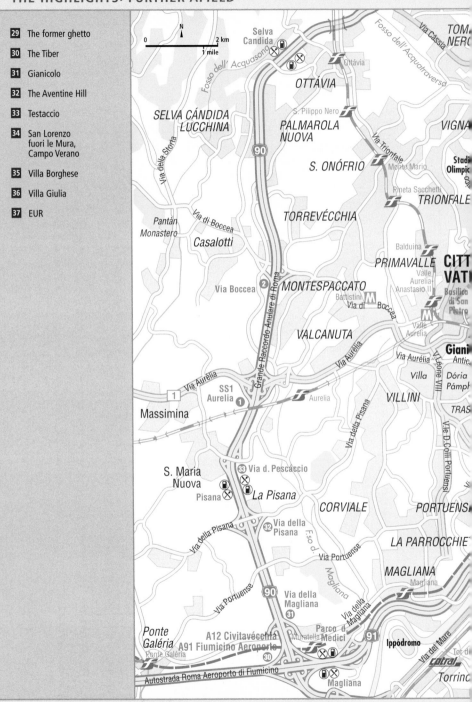

Grande Raccordo Anulare di Roma

90

Prato Láuro

Nomentana

11

F.so Lucia

cotral
Grottarossa
Aeroporto dell'Urbe

Via Salária

Nuovo Salario

V. D. Prati Fiscali

V. S.Alessandro

12

cotral
Tor di Quinto

Ippódromo di Tor di Quinto

Viale Jónio

Via Adriatico

TUFELLO

Via Nomentana

Settecamini

Via Tiburtina

Italico

Centro Sportivo Acqua Acetosa

cotral
Monte Antenne

Circ. Salária

Nomentana

MONTE SACRO

S. BASÍLIO

SS5 Tiburtina

13

Campi sportivi
VIO

cotral

REBIBBIA

5

A24
L'Aquila/Pescara

Rebibbia

14

Via Salária

Villa Ada

Piazza Euclide

PARIOLI

F. Aniene

PIETRALATA

La Rustica N.

LA RUSTICA

Viale B. Buozzi

Via Nomentana

Via d. Monti Tiburtini

Circ. Nomentana

La Rústica

F.so

36 Villa Giulia

Staz. Tiburtina

S. MARIA D. SOCCORO

24

Via Tiburtina

la Rústica

35 Villa Borghese

C.so d'Italia

Tiburtina

Tor Sapienza

15

Corso

Città Universitaria

Via Tiburtina

Via Togliatti

TOR SAPIENZA

SP Prenestina

San Lorenzo fuori le Mura

34 Campo Verano

Via Fiorentini

16

Roma
Termini F.S.

Prenestina

Tiburtina

Viale Palmiro Togliatti

Via Prenestina

29 The former ghetto

Via Labicana

Via Prenestina

Tor Bella Mónaca

17

Colosseo

Basílica S. Giovanni in Laterano

Dives in Misericordia

32 The Aventine Hill

Tuscolana

Alessi

cotral

TUSCOLANO

90

Terme di Caracalla

Via Appia Nuova

CENTOCELLE

cotral

Testaccio

Via Casilina

Via Tuscolana

Tor Pignattara

cotral
Centocelle

Casilina

Ostiense

Santa Maria in Palmis (Domine Quo vadis?)

Via Casilina

Togliatti

Via Casilina

cotral

Torrenova

TORRE MAURA

18

SS6 Casilina

iber

cotral

GARBA-TELLA

Catacombe di S. Callisto

QUADRARO

TORRE NOVA

19

A1 Nápoli

TIENSE

S. Paolo

Via Ardeatina

Tempio di Romolo

1d

E 45

Tuscolana

Via Cristoforo

Fiera Campionaria di Roma

San Sebastiano e Catacombe

la Romanina

20

SS215 Tuscolana

Torrenova

Ardeatino

Parco Reg.

CINECITTÀ

Anagnina

21

Tuscolana

R

L'Annunziatella

Quarto Miglio

Capanelle

22

SS511 Anagnina

215

Via Tuscolana

Ponte Linari

Via Laurentina

Statuário

Via Appia Nuova

511

Via Tuscolana

M

Laurentina

Capanelle

Acquedotto dei Quintili

Ippódromo

rf

Cecchignola

dell'Appia Antica

Grande Raccordo Anulare di Roma

MORENA

THE HIGHLIGHTS: FURTHER AFIELD

The area around the Via del Portico d'Ottavia is characterized by picturesque courtyards and restaurants. The Jewish population of Rome was once confined here. Small images below, from left: The Fontana delle Tartarughe (fountain of the tortoises) in the Piazza Mattei; sculpture in a rear courtyard; busts on the Casa di Lorenzo Manilio.

TIP Boccione

This Jewish bakery is famous for its cakes made from traditional recipes: try the *Torta di Ricotta* (cheesecake) with chocolate or berries.

Via del Portico d'Ottavia 1; Tel 06 687 86 37; daily except Saturday; Tram 8.

For many years, Roman Jews suffered little repression, but in 1555 they were forced by Pope Paul V to resettle in a particularly unhealthy area on the banks of the Tiber. The Jewish ghetto's population numbered around 4,000, all crammed onto a small piece of land surrounded by a high wall. Life was difficult and when the Tiber flooded, the people were forced to vacate the lower floors of their tenements. A curfew was in operation, forcing them to remain in the ghetto at night and certain professions were forbidden. On Sundays they were forced to listen to a Christian priest – this degrading practice ending in 1848. However, the ghetto itself remained until the pope lost his secular authority over Rome in 1870. As a symbolic gesture, the new city government had the ghetto wall torn down. The Portico d'Ottavia, in the heart of the former ghetto, dates from the 2nd century BC. Emperor Augustus had it redesigned and dedicated to his sister Octavia.

THE HIGHLIGHTS: FURTHER AFIELD

INFO Boat trips on the Tiber

For Rome, originally founded where the Tiber flows around in a bend at the so-called "knee", the Tiber was crucial for trade and commerce. Small image, below left: Brave (or foolhardy) young Romans traditionally celebrate the New Year by jumping in the river. Right: The Tiber as a symbolic fountain figure in the Piazza del Campidoglio.

See Rome's historic monuments from a different perspective – the pleasure boat trip lasts a good hour and runs between the Ponte Marconi and the Ponte Duca d'Aosta.

Trips start from the Ponte Sant'Angelo (near the Castel Sant'Angelo); Tel 06 78 93 61; Bus 40, 64.

The Tiber, cloudy and grey, flows erratically and "often causes great damage". This was the harsh verdict of Swiss scholar Johann Jacob Grasser in an early travel guide in 1609. The third-longest river in Italy, the Tiber's source is in the Apennines and it drains into the Tyrrhenian Sea. In order to control its flow – or overflow, as it flooded regularly – in the 1870s high embankments were constructed. Despite having had its excesses tamed, the Tiber has still not lost any of its magic, and a walk along its banks is a treat on a warm evening – perhaps to the Ponte Fabricio, one of the oldest bridges in the city. This leads to the Isola Tiberina, an island lying in the river like a ship at anchor opposite what used to be the old port of Ostia. After an epidemic in 291 BC, a temple was erected on the island, dedicated to Aesculapius, the god of healing. The church of San Bartolomeo was built on the ruins of this pagan place of worship in the 10th century.

Street scenes in Trastevere (images, below right). Large image: Santa Maria is supposedly the oldest sacred Christian building in Rome. According to legend, the church was founded in the 3rd century; the façade, however, was restored by Italian baroque architect Carlo Fontana at the turn of the 18th century. Small images, right: The popular Sunday flea market at the Porta Portese; an instrument maker on Vicolo del Cedre.

THE "OTHER" ROME

Named after the Roman god Janus, Gianicolo (the Janiculum Hill) lies on the west bank of the Tiber. The Aurelian Wall was extended up the hill to keep the water mills on the Gianicolo that were used to grind corn within the confines of the city. Despite not being one of the classic seven hills of Rome, it has witnessed its share of significant historical events. In 1849, the national hero Giuseppe Garibaldi barricaded himself here against French troops, who crushed the short-lived Roman republic. Memorials to these conflicts, which were precursors to the unification of Italy, show Garibaldi on horseback, looking toward the Vatican and his wife Anita, also on horseback, a baby in one hand and a gun in the other. These monuments are in marked contrast to their idyllic, leafy surroundings. The hill is much loved by locals and offers superb views over the city. A canon is fired from the hill at noon each day to mark the exact time.

THE HIGHLIGHTS: FURTHER AFIELD

According to legend, the basilica of Santa Sabina (large image, below left) was founded in AD 425 on the site of a house belonging to Sabina, a rich Roman woman who converted to Christianity. Large image, below right: A fountain head in the inner courtyard of Santa Sabina. Right: Pines make the Aventine Hill a green oasis.

TIP Pizzeria Remo

One of Rome's best-loved pizzerias. The pizzas are thin, large and crispy. After 20.00, you may have to wait to enjoy them – but it will be worth it.

Piazza Santa Maria Liberatrice 44; Tel 06 574 62 70; Mon–Sat 19.00–1.00; Tram 3.

The Aventine is the southernmost of the seven hills of Rome: its western slope runs down to the Tiber, from where there's a wonderful view of the Isola Tiberina and the Vatican on the other side of the river. At the top of the hill, crowned by the 5th-century basilica of Santa Sabina, the hectic life of the city seems far away, which is why it is one of the most popular residential areas in Rome. The Aventine Hill was initially occupied by merchants, who carried out their business on the quays along the Tiber; then the area became chic and the rich and famous built villas here. Emperor Hadrian lived on the Aventine before he rose to become the ruler of the Roman Empire. Between the Aventine and Testaccio is the Protestant cemetery, where many members of the foreign community were buried after dying in Italy – including English Romantic poets John Keats and Percy Bysshe Shelley who drowned off Livorno.

Modern graffiti on the old walls of Ex Mattatoio in Testaccio (large image, below left), the lively, traditional area beneath the artificial hill of the same name. The slaughterhouse opened in 1891 – today it is home to the city's experimental artists; concerts are held here, as are craft and food markets. Right: food sellers in Testaccio.

TIP Checchino dal 1887

Owned by the Mariani family for generations, this restaurant specializes in offal, including calves' heads and pigs' trotters, as well as more standard Roman dishes.

*Via di Monte Testaccio 30;
Tel 06 574 63 18; Tues–Sat
12.30–15.00 and 20.00–24.00;
Metro B Piramide, Bus 75.*

Monte Testaccio, around 35 m (114 feet) high and located in the working-class area of the same name, is actually an artificial mound almost entirely composed of the broken remains of amphorae (*testae* in Latin) accumulated over the centuries. Amphorae were large clay pots used to store and transport food and wine from the nearby Tiber port, which disappeared long ago. In the 19th century, the hill was a place of pilgrimage, and its summit is still crowned by a cross. Monte Testaccio is now officially barred to visitors, as amateur archeologists found the opportunity to take a fragment or two home a little too tempting. In the 19th century, Testaccio was a residential area for workers at the gas works and the slaughterhouse. Since then, the area has become a trendy meeting place with restaurants, bars, discos, and cultural events. Many of these take place in the former slaughterhouse, Ex Mattatoio, at the foot of the hill.

THE HIGHLIGHTS: FURTHER AFIELD

Designated as Rome's municipal cemetery, the vast Campo Verano is worth a visit for its elaborate tombs, mausoleums, and monuments. Garibaldi is buried here along with thousands of others. Right: The cloisters of San Lorenzo fuori le Mura. After St Laurence was tortured to death and buried here, his tomb became a place of pilgrimage.

TIP Rive Gauche 2

A fashionable spot for night owls, with a successful mix of discotheque and café, in the heart of the student quarter of San Lorenzo.

*Via dei Sabelli 43;
Tel 06 445 67 22; 18.00–2.00,
daily; Tram 3.*

The district of San Lorenzo, just outside Rome's eastern walls, suffered serious bomb damage during World War II. The basilica of the same name – dedicated to St Laurence, who died a martyr's death for his faith in 258 – was also damaged, but has been restored. It was founded during the reign of the emperor Constantine (4th century), but has been altered and extended many times since then. Today's San Lorenzo fuori le Mura was formed when the existing St Laurence's church was joined with an adjacent church dedicated to the Virgin Mary. The relics of St Laurence and other saints are stored here; San Lorenzo also houses the sarcophagus of Pius IX who died in 1878; often regarded as the first modern pope, he was the last ruler of the independent Papal States, before the papacy was reduced to a spiritual force. Founded at the beginning of the 19th century, the adjacent Campo Verano cemetery is the largest in Rome.

THE HIGHLIGHTS: FURTHER AFIELD

A triumph of *trompe l'oeil*: the ceiling in the entrance hall of the Villa Borghese (large image). Small images, below: Bernini's *David* (middle) and (from top) *Pluto and Proserpina*, Canova's *Paolina Borghese*, and *Sleeping Hermaphrodite*, a Roman copy of a Greek sculpture. Small image, right: caryatids and Etruscan treasures in the Villa Giulia.

TIP Margutta RistorArte

Outside the park of the Villa Borghese, south of the Piazza del Popolo, is Rome's first vegetarian restaurant. Temporary exhibitions show works by young local artists.

Via Margutta 118; Tel 06 32 65 05 77; 12.30–15.30 and 19.30–23.30, daily; Metro A Spagna, Flaminio.

These two villas on the northern edge of the city are really worth seeing, not just because of their architectural beauty but also because of their spectacular art collections. Villa Giulia, built between 1551 and 1553 and used by Pope Julius III as a summer palace, once housed the pope's collection of statues; in 1555, they were taken to the Vatican, filling 160 boats. Today it is the home of a world-class Etruscan Museum. The Villa Borghese, built between 1613 and 1616, was once owned by Cardinal Scipione Borghese, an important patron of the arts. Many statues created for him by Bernini are on display here, together with world-famous works by other artists – such as Titian's *Sacred and Profane Love*. The villas are set in sumptuous gardens, landscaped in the naturalistic English manner, and a work of art in themselves (see p. 168). There is a also a small zoo with natural barriers rather than cages housing many endangered species.

Mussolini's *urbs magna*, a fascist mega-lopolis, was supposed to recall the ancient Roman Empire. The most striking structure is the Palazzo della Civiltà del Lavoro, known as "the square Colosseum" by locals (large image). Typical of fascist architecture, the palazzo is faced with travertine marble; statues represent the arts and different trades.

This fascinating museum uses models of ancient Rome at a scale of 1:250 to tell the story of the city's past, housed in a building donated to the city by the Fiat company.
*Piazza Giovanni Agnelli 10;
Tel 06 592 60 41; Tues–Sat
9.00–18.15, Sun 9.00–13.30;
Metro B EUR Fermi.*

As an exercise to display the glory of fascism, the EUR never quite came to fruition. Mussolini planned a World Exhibition for 1942, set in the southern part of Rome, with residential areas, museums, and parks. World War II intervened, and although the Esposizione Universale di Roma (EUR), the Universal Rome Exhibition, never materialized, by 1938 construction was already well underway. Inevitably, as with many projects pursued by Mussolini, existing buildings made way for the new. The most notable building in the EUR – today a popular residential and business area – is the Palazzo della Civiltà del Lavoro, nicknamed "the square Colosseum". It is proof of Mussolini's desire to link his state with the great ancient Roman Empire. The complex now contains a large sports arena, the Pala Lottomatica, built for the 1960 Summer Olympics, the National Museum of Prehistory and Ethnography, and the Museum of Roman Civilization.

Legendary passion: Marcello Mastroianni and Anita Ekberg in *La dolce vita* (large images, below). It was the first film Mastroianni made with Fellini. Subsequently, he became a kind of dramatic alter ego for the director. Right, from left: Film stars Giulietta Masina; Anna Magnani; and Sophia Loren; and the director and actor Roberto Benigni.

CINECITTÀ – THE ROMAN DREAM FACTOR

Some 20 km (12 miles) south of the city, lies the famous Cinecittà film studio complex, built on the orders of Mussolini in 1937. It covers approximately 600,000 sq m (717,600 sq yards). Vast water tanks enable film production companies to recreate sea battles – just as the ancient Romans did when they flooded the Colosseum and the Piazza Navona, creating artificial lakes for the same purpose. In 1997, Cinecittà was privatized by the Italian government, and today is owned by a holding company. Legendary films shot in the studios include Federico Fellini's *La dolce vita* (1960), starring Marcello Mastroianni and Anita Ekberg, about the dark side of Roman high society, the meaning of life – and love. In Fellini's *Roma* (1972), the city itself is the subject of the film, with Anna Magnani – a native Roman, playing her last role. The 1950s saw the production of the epic *Ben Hur* with its famous chariot race, while more recently Martin Scorsese's *The Gangs of New York* was shot here, as was Mel Gibson's controversial *The Passion of Christ*. The studios are also used by international TV companies such as the BBC and HBO. In 2007 fire broke out and destroyed parts of the film studios, but was fortunately contained by Italian firefighters who worked throughout the night. They managed to save the oldest parts of the studio, where classics such as *Ben Hur* and many of Fellini's most notable films were made.

BEYOND ROME

Even in ancient times, the Romans felt the need, particularly in summer, to escape from the city. Those who could afford it bought themselves a villa in the country, where they could relax and recoup their energies – Cicero's estate at Tusculum was famous. These days, there is an exodus from the city on public holidays: the inhabitants of the Italian capital are doubly privileged in that they have the sea on their doorstep to one side and the open countryside, the *campagna*, and the mountains on the other. The nearest sea to Rome is at Ostia – not the ancient port of Ostia Antica, now silted up and no longer on the coast, but the resort of modern Ostia on the Tyrrhenian Sea.

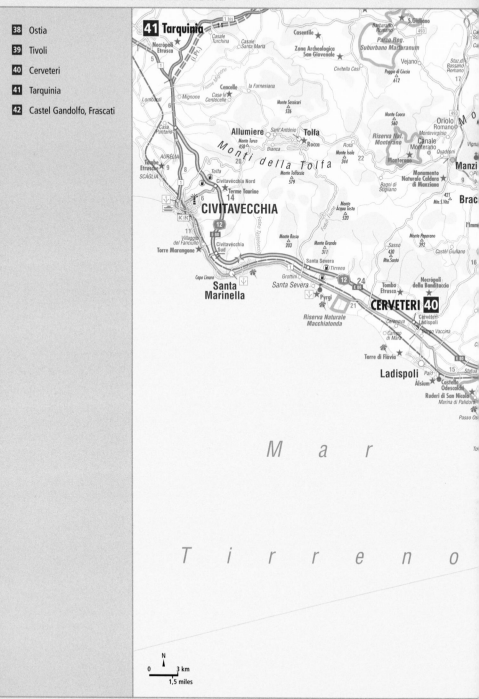

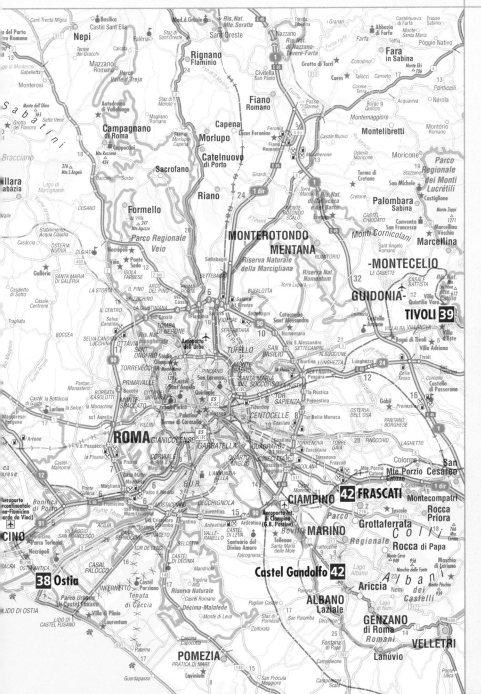

THE HIGHLIGHTS: BEYOND ROME

TIP La Vecchia Pineta

As Rome's suburb and seaside resort, people flocked to the fashionable Lido di Ostia to escape the oppressive summer heat of the city in the 1950s and 1960s. Its nightclubs were full of the smart set and film stars but its charm eventually faded and the visitor numbers declined. But Ostia is now becoming chic again and *La dolce vita* has returned.

A fish restaurant much loved by locals and tourists alike, with a terrace above the beach, where you can enjoy seafood and a glass of chilled Frascati or Orvieto.

*Lungomare/Piazzale
dell'Aquilone 4;
Tel 06 56 47 02 55; daily.*

Ostia Antica, the trading and naval port of ancient Rome, was built in the 4th and 3rd centuries BC around 25 km (15 miles) south of Rome. Originally situated on the coast at the mouth of the Tiber, the site is now 3 km (2 miles) inland due to the silting up of the area. Excavations revealed that the city flourished for many centuries with magnificent houses, markets, public baths, taverns, sports complexes, and a playhouse – many of its buildings have been very well preserved and can still be seen today. The gradual silting up of the port contributed to its decline and it was abandoned in the 9th century. Work began on reclaiming coastal land in 1883 and modern Ostia (also known as Lido de Roma) was founded in 1908. Mussolini ensured Rome could easily access its new suburb by building a new road and there is also a rail link, the journey taking around 30 minutes. In 1976 Ostia officially became the XIII *municipio* of the commune of Rome.

THE HIGHLIGHTS:
BEYOND ROME

TIP Antica Osteria dei Carrettieri

Tivoli is best known for its two UNESCO World Heritage Sites: Hadrian's Villa (small image, right and large image, far right), (AD 117–134), is a perfect example of Roman elegance and opulence; the Renaissaince Villa d'Este (all other images) is noted for its spectacular gardens, with elaborate water cascades, fountains, pools, and troughs.

A good restaurant in Tivoli, ideal for a meal to build up your strength before visiting the Villa d'Este and the Villa Adriana.

Via Domenico Giuliani 55;
Tel 07 74 33 01 59;
daily except Wed.

Tivoli has been Rome's summer resort for over 2,000 years. Thanks to its position in the Monti Tiburtini, some 30 km (19 miles) from the city, the air here was always fresh and there were healing springs with mineral-rich waters. Finding it much easier to sleep in Tivoli, the Emperor Augustus had a villa built here, while Hadrian's Villa Adriana is located 6 km (4 miles) to the south. It includes a pool lined with columns and an artificial grotto, a refuge where the emperor could pursue his love of painting. In the Renaissance era, with the renewed interest in ancient times, the resort underwent a revival. One of the most impressive palaces dating from this period is the Villa d'Este, famed for its terraced gardens, while the Villa Gregoriana is located in a deep valley through which the Aniene River courses down in spectacular fashion over several waterfalls, culminating in the Grande Cascata, which falls 108 m (356 feet).

THE HIGHLIGHTS:
BEYOND ROME

The Greek influence on Etruscan culture can mainly be seen in their sculpture. Small images, right and below: Etruscan sculptures and a Greek vase from Cerveteri. Large images, below: Sarcophagi in the National Museum housed in the Palazzo Vitelleschi in the medieval town of Tarquinia; and a dancer from the "Priest's Tomb" in Tarquinia.

TIP Antica Locanda le Ginestre

Located next to the Museo Nazionale di Cerveteri, this is one of the best restaurants in Lazio. It serves delicious meals made mainly from locally sourced produce. Reservation recommended at weekends.

Piazza Santa Maria 5;
Tel 06 994 06 72; Tues–Sun.

Situated in the modern provinces of Rome and Viterbo, the towns of Cerveteri and Tarquinia are famous for their superb Etruscan necropolises for which they have been jointly declared a World Heitage Site. The tombs, which show the different burial practices of the earliest civilizations of the northern Mediter-

ranean area, depict the everyday lives of the people who lived here. Cerveteri is famous for the architecture and sculpture of its tombs, with a variety of forms – some carved from the rock and topped with burial mounds, with corridors and rooms showing structural detail that gives an idea of Etruscan home life and

decor. Other square-shaped tombs are laid out in streets with small courtyards like a small town. The tombs at Tarquinia are best known for their frescoes depicting banquets, dancing, and hunting scenes. Many of the 6,000 tombs are yet to be excavated – so far some 200 painted tombs have been found.

TIP Gardens of the Villa Aldobrandini

Fountains and water features decorate the gardens of the Villa Aldobrandini in Frascati (large images, below and right). The present building (not open to the public) dates from the early 17th century, while the imposing façade is 18th century. Small image, below: The papal palace at Castel Gandolfo, the pope's summer residence.

It's a short train journey to Frascati, 20 km (12 miles) south of Rome, famous not just for its white wine, but also for its villas and their gardens, including the Villa Aldobrandini.
Tourist Office, Piazzale Marconi 1; Tel 06 942 03 31; Apr–Sept Mon–Fri 9.00-13.00, 15.00–18.00; Oct–Mar 9.00–13.00, 15.00–17.00.

Castel Gandolfo is a small town on the edge of a crater lake in the Colli Albani (Alban Hills), on the site of the ancient city of Alba Longa, founded some time after 1150 BC and destroyed by the Romans. Castel Gandolfo is best known for being the papal summer residence – even the pope has to have his house in the country. The Catholic Church purchased the *castello* toward the end of the 16th century and in 1628 Pope Urban VIII had a villa constructed on the site by Maderno. The country seat of Emperor Domitian (around AD 90) was also located here. Castel Gandolfo is not open to the public. Frascati, north of Castel Gandolfo, was a holiday resort for the Roman *jeunesse dorée* in ancient times. Today it is known not only for its villas dating from the 16th and 17th centuries – such as Villa Aldobrandini – but also for the crisp white wine that is cultivated in the area.

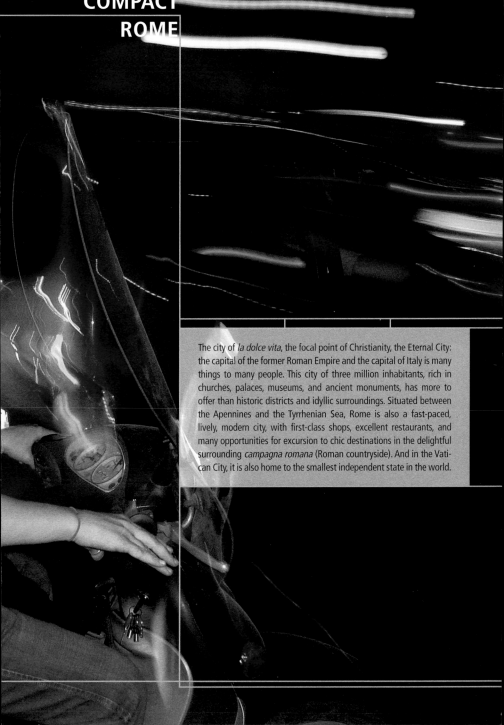

COMPACT ROME

The city of *la dolce vita*, the focal point of Christianity, the Eternal City: the capital of the former Roman Empire and the capital of Italy is many things to many people. This city of three million inhabitants, rich in churches, palaces, museums, and ancient monuments, has more to offer than historic districts and idyllic surroundings. Situated between the Apennines and the Tyrrhenian Sea, Rome is also a fast-paced, lively, modern city, with first-class shops, excellent restaurants, and many opportunities for excursion to chic destinations in the delightful surrounding *campagna romana* (Roman countryside). And in the Vatican City, it is also home to the smallest independent state in the world.

Along with Milan and Turin, Rome is a hub of Italian fashion.

Museums, music, and drama

Ara Pacis
The great Altar of Peace of Emperor Augustus was dedicated in 9 BC and has a number of finely sculpted reliefs in white marble. It is now located within a museum complex designed by the architect Richard Meier.
Lungotevere in Augusta; Tel 06 82 05 91 27; Tues–Sun 9.00–19.00. www.arapacis.it

Galleria Colonna
These sumptuous apartments in the Palazzo Colonna are well worth a visit. The extensive collection of paintings and sculptures assembled by the Colonna family includes works by masters such as Tintoretto, Annibale Carracci, Rubens, Pietro da Cortona, Anthony van Dyck, and many others.
Via Pilotta 17; Tel 06 678 43 50; Sat 09.00–13.00. www.galleriacolonna.it

Galleria dell'Accademia Nazionale di San Luca
Founded in 1593, the academy promotes the arts of painting, sculpture, and architecture; the gallery has over 500 portraits and numerous other paintings and sculptures, including superb works by Canova, Raphael, Rubens, and van Dyck.
Piazza dell'Accademia di San Luca 77; Tel 06 679 88 48; Mon–Sat 9.00–13.00. www.accademiasanluca.it

Galleria Doria Pamphili
The private collection of the Pamphili family, which was started in 1650, boasts significant works by Titian, Caravaggio, Annibale Carracci, Velázquez, Claude Lorrain, Pieter Brueghel the Elder, and others. The paintings are displayed hung one above the other, in a layout typical of baroque collections.
Piazza del Collegio Romano 1a; Tel 06 679 73 23; Fri–Wed 10.00–17.00. www.doriapamphilj.it

Galleria Spada
This collection housed in the Palazzo Spada, acquired by Cardinal Bernardino Spada, includes antiquities and paintings by Titian, Reni, Guercino, and Gentileschi, among others. It is now owned by the state. The Galleria Prospettiva, a peristyle by Francesco Borromini in the palace courtyard, is also worth a visit.
Piazza Capo di Ferro 3; Tel 06 686 11 58; Tues–Sun 9.00–19.00. www.beniculturalionline.it

Keats-Shelley House
Near the Spanish Steps, in a former artists' quarter once inhabited by many British expatriates, this museum is dedicated to the poet John Keats, who died here in 1821, aged 25, of tuberculosis. The exterior is just as it was in the time of the British Romantic poets. It also contains mementoes of Shelley, Lord Byron, and other British literary figures such as Wordsworth, Browning, and Wilde.
Piazza di Spagna 26; Tel 06 678 42 35; Mon–Fri 9.00–13.00 and 15.00–18.00, Sat 11.00–14.00 and 15.00–18.00. www.keats-shelley-house.org

Museo Barracco
Located in a 16th-century palace designed by Antonio da Sangallo the Younger, these ancient works of art from around the Mediterranean area were collected by Giovanni Barracco.
Corso Vittorio Emanuele II 168; Tel 06 68 80 68 48; Tues–Sun 9.00–19.00. www.museobarracco.it

Museo Nazionale Etrusco di Villa Giulia
Founded in 1889 and housed in a mannerist villa, this museum has superb Etruscan objects, as well as an important collection of Greek vases.
Piazzale Villa Giulia 9; Tel 06 320 19 51; Tues–Sun 8.30–19.30. www.archeologia. beniculturali.it

Festivals and events

Natale di Roma
The founding of the city is celebrated at different locations throughout the city, but mainly at the Piazza del Campidoglio. Bands play, and people in historical costumes re-enact scenes from the city's history. The festivities conclude with a magnificent firework display.
Tel 06 51 60 79 51; 19–21 April. www.gsr-roma.com

Piazza Navona Christmas market
Every year the square hosts a seasonal market filled with stalls selling handmade toys, nativity scenes, decorations, gifts, and food and drink. As dusk descends the lights create a delightful atmosphere. Who needs snow!
Piazza Navona; Mid December to 6 January.

Sport and leisure

City tours on bus 110
If you are new to Rome and want to gain a first impression of its highlights and overall layout, a good starting point is a trip on the 110, the open-top sightseeing bus. The tour starts near the Termini station and there are ten stops at which you can get off if you wish to take a closer look at any of the historical monuments along the route. If you remain on the bus, the tour takes a good 2 hours.
Piazza del Cinquecento in front of Stazione Termini; Tel 06 684 09 01; daily. www.trambusopen.com

Museo Nazionale delle Paste Alimentari
What would Roman and Italian cuisine be without its staple dish pasta? In this museum you can find out everything you could want to know about pasta. It's a good place to visit in the morning

From left: The Fontana del Moro in the Piazza Navona; the Piazza della Rotonda with the portico of the Pantheon; *ciabatta e pane*; nipping through the alleys of Rome on a moped.

CENTRO STORICO

This section contains additional insider tips on places to visit, restaurants, accommodation, nightlife, and festivals and events, supplementing the information given in the "The Highlights" section (pp. 28–55).

Santa Maria dei Miracoli: ceiling fresco.

so that you can give yourself an appetite for lunch. Audio guides in English are available at the entrance.
Piazza Scanderbeg 117,
Tel 06 699 11 19;
9.30–17.30, daily.
www.museodellapasta.it

Spas

Tevere Village
Sun-lovers need not miss out in the heart of the city. With a fantastic view of St Peter's, this is a good spot right by the Tiber, between the Piazza Navona and the Castel Sant' Angelo, in which to hire a sunlounger and parasol. There are swimming pools for cooling off, and if you want something more strenuous, you can work out in the fitness area.

Shopping

Angelo Vitti Atelier
Angelo Vitti's exclusive designs for women are on sale in this shop situated not far from the Spanish Steps and the Palazzo del Quirinale. Good window shopping for fashion fans, but only those with bulging bank accounts will be able to buy.
Via Gregoriana 45/46;
Tel 06 678 08 20.
www.angelovitti.it

Annibale Gammarelli
This somewhat unassuming tailor's shop has been exclusively responsible for supplying the pope's robes for over 200 years. It also produces distinguished clerical vestments for anyone – priests or the general public alike – who should want or require them.
Via di Santa Chiara 34;
Tel 06 68 80 13 14.

Enoteca Buccone
A legendary wine, vinegar, and oil shop located in a former stable block. Selection is made somewhat easier if you have fortified yourself with one of the small, tasty snacks on offer first.
Via Ripetta 19/20;
Tel 06 361 21 54;
Mon–Thurs midday, Fri, Sat midday and evenings.
www.enotecabuccone.com

Fanshop AS Roma
As the finances of football club Associazione Sportiva Roma could do with a boost, this shop hopes to add to the contents of its coffers by selling the usual club paraphernalia, as well as tickets for the "Giallorossi" (yellow-red) matches.
Piazza Colonna 360;
Tel 06 678 65 14.
www.asromastore.it

Ferrari Store
Everything to do with Ferrari, one of Italy's national institutions, and its iconic and (generally) red Italian sports car. The only things you can't buy here are the cars themselves.
Via Tomacelli 147;
Tel 06 689 29 79;
Mon–Sat 10.00–19.30, Sun from 11.00.
www.romecity.it/ Ferraristore.htm

The Lion Bookshop
Founded in 1947, this bookstore has over 30,000 titles in English on its shelves, covering fiction and non-fiction, for adults and children, and with in-depth specialist sections. The atmosphere is friendly and there is a small café serving bagels, cookies, and cakes. It is situated close to the Spanish Steps and the Piazza del Popolo.
Via dei Greci 36;
Tel 06 3265 4007/06 3265 0437.
www.thelionbookshop.com

La Cicogna
A shopping paradise for mothers and expectant mums with cash to spare. Maternity fashion and a large selection of somewhat extravagant children's clothes, not necessarily for everyday use, are available. There's usually a small selection of items at reduced prices at "The Stork" (*la cicogna*).
Via Frattina 138;
Tel 06 679 19 12.

La Soffitta sotto i Portici
A monthly market with paintings, graphic art, engravings, ceramics, and porcelain, as well as secondhand items, clocks, and furniture; worth browsing, as you might well find a bargain. There are around 100 stalls.
Piazza Augusto Imperatore; every third Sunday in the month; 10.00 until twilight.

Max Mara
Visitors who are already familiar with Max Mara's women's fashion may enjoy a visit to one of its Italian outlets. The sales assistants are friendly, there's a wide range of clothing, and the prices are reasonable. Achille Maramotti founded his ready-to-wear empire in Rome in 1951 – the label became famous for its classic cutting and simple lines.
Via Frattina 28;
Tel 06 679 36 38.

Mercato delle Stampe
An enormous selection of antiquarian and art books, as well as good-quality prints and engravings.
Piazza Borghese;
Mon–Fri 9.00–17.30, Sat, Sun 9.00–19.00, closed Aug.

Mercato di Piazza delle Coppelle
A photogenic and lively fruit, vegetable, and flower market close to the Pantheon.
Piazza delle Coppelle;
Mon–Sat 7.00–13.00.

Only Hearts
American designer Jean Frances Ottaviano has three shops in Rome – the only city in Europe in which she has a base – selling original fashion at reasonable prices. Underwear, bags, and T-shirts are in particular demand.
Piazza della Chiesa Nuova 21; Tel 06 686 46 47;
Tues–Sat 10.00–20.00, Sun–Mon 12.00–20.00.
www.onlyhearts.com

The Sala degli Ambasciatori in the Palazzo del Quirinale.

Salvatore Ferragamo

Italian shoe designer Salvatore Ferragamo began his career producing *scarpe belle* (beautiful shoes) for film productions in Hollywood in the 1920s. He died in 1960 but the company he founded now makes luxury goods that are well renowned all over the world, including the finest leather purses, bags, and ladies' and men's shoes on sale in these two almost adjacent shops.
Via Condotti 65 and 73/74;
Tel 06 678 11 30 and
06 679 15 65.
www.salvatoreferragamo.it

Eating and drinking

Cinque Lune

A traditional small *pasticceria* popular with all age groups, with a wonderful selection of pastries, near the Piazza Navona.
Corso del Rinascimento;
Tel 06 880 10 05,
Tues–Sun 8.00–21.30.

Ditirambo

Close to the Campo de' Fiori, this restaurant, reminiscent of a French bistro, serves creative Roman cuisine using the freshest ingredients. The pasta, bread, and desserts are all homemade, and wines come from all over Italy.

Piazza della Cancelleria 74,
Tel 06 87 16 26.
www.ristoranteditirambo.com

Enoteca Cul de Sac

This restaurant offers excellent Roman cuisine with an enormous selection of the best wines to accompany it.
Piazza Pasquino 73;
Tel 06 58 33 39 20.

Hard Rock Café Rome

A Roman outpost of the famous international restaurant chain; dine in a room decorated with all kinds of rock memorabilia – guitars, stage clothing, photographs, and gold records.
Via Vittorio Veneto 62 a/b;
Tel 06 420 30 51;
Restaurant: Sun–Thurs 12.00–24.00, Fri–Sat 12.00–1.00; Bar: Sun–Thurs 12.00–1.30, Fri–Sat 12.00–2.00.
www.hardrock.com

Il Margutta RistorArte

One of the best and most sophisticated vegetarian restaurants to open in Rome and even Italy for almost 30 years. And it's not just the meals that are delicious – the locally grown organic wines are too. On Saturdays, a live band plays, and there's a jazz band on the last Tuesday of the month.

Via Margutta 118;
Tel 06 32 65 05 77;
12.30–15.30 and
19.30–23.30 daily.
www.ilmargutta.it

La Penna d'Oca

A snug, sophisticated restaurant offering some outstanding dishes. Located just south of Piazza del Popolo and not far from the gardens of the Villa Borghese, fish features largely on the menu – a fond homage to the owner's Sardinian roots.
Via della Penna 53;
Tel 06 320 28 98.

La Rosetta

Founded in 1966, and highly praised in the Italian press, this family-run fish restaurant near the Pantheon is the best of its kind in Rome, perhaps even the best in Italy. The dishes have a Sicilian slant, often simple but extremely delicious. The fish is freshly caught from the waters off the ports of Lazio, Anzio, Civitavecchia, and Terracina. Smart dress and reservations are essential.
Via della Rosetta 8;
Tel 06 686 10 02;
Mon–Sat lunch and dinner.
www.larosetta.com

Le Jardin de Russie

Perhaps the most beautiful five-star hotel in the city, Hotel de Russie boasts a first-class restaurant with beautiful terraced gardens. The Mediterranean and international cuisine makes the most of the excellent local produce on offer.
Via del Babuino 9;
Tel 06 32 88 88 70;
7.00–10.30, 12.30–14.30 and 19.30–22.30, daily.
www.hotelderussie.it

L'Orso 80

A pleasant restaurant with a good selection of antipasti and delicious meat, fish, and pasta dishes – all at reasonable prices.
Via dell'Orso 33;
Tel 06 86 49 04.

Nino

A classic Italian restaurant located near the Spanish Steps, with a charming atmosphere and a Tuscan slant. Much frequented by the Romans themselves – and sometimes by movie stars such as Jennifer Lopez, Brooke Shields, and Jim Carrey among others, who helped celebrity couple Tom Cruise and Katie Holmes celebrate their wedding here.
Via Borgognona 11;
Tel 06 678 67 52.

Accommodation

Casa Howard

Rome pulses with life around the Spanish Steps, and though the two beautiful Casa Howard boutique hotels are close by, they are still a relatively well-kept secret. The Via Capo le Case hotel, opened in 2000, was carefully created with great attention to detail by owner Jenifer Howard Forneris. Interior designer Tommaso Ziffer, who also made his mark in the Hotel de Russie, has created a stylish hotel at Via Sistina. You can choose to have breakfast served in your room, and after a strenuous day sightseeing, the small Turkish bath offers some peace and relaxation.
Via Capo le Case 18 and Via Sistina 149;
Tel 06 69 92 45 55.
www.casahoward.com

From left: The monument to Victor Emmanuel II in the Piazza Venezia; the Altar of Peace of Emperor Augustus; the exterior of the Palazzo del Quirinale; the historic flower market on the Campo de' Fiori.

CENTRO STORICO

This section contains additional insider tips on places to visit, restaurants, accommodation, nightlife, and festivals and events, supplementing the information given in the "The Highlights" section (pp. 28–55).

Restored *putti* in a shop near the Campo de' Fiori.

De Russie

A high-class hotel located not far from the Spanish Steps and the Piazza del Popolo, with a highly recommended gourmet restaurant, a stylish spa, and a beautifully laid out garden. An oasis of wellbeing in the very heart of the Eternal City.
Via del Babuino 9;
Tel 06 32 88 81.
www.hotelderussie.it

Eden

This top international hotel in a traditional style is one of the best addresses in Rome. The rooms and suites are luxuriously furnished with antiques and fine marble baths, with politicians and well-known Italian stage stars among the regular clientele. The view from the roof terrace is superb. The La Terrazza restaurant is considered one of the best in the city, but, unsurprisingly, the prices are correspondingly high.
Via Ludovisi 49;
Tel 06 47 81 21.
www.hotel-eden.it

Hassler Villa Medici

A first-class hotel, in a superb location above the Spanish Steps. The interior and facilities are appropriately luxurious: marble baths and antiques are a feature of the

comfortable rooms, and the service is excellent. The Hassler is also the much-loved residence of the Swedish royal couple (the Queen Silvia Suite). The hotel also boasts a good restaurant as well as an incomparable view over one of the most beautiful squares in Rome.
Piazza Trinità dei Monti 6;
Tel 06 69 93 40.
www.hotelhasslerroma.com

Hotel d'Inghilterra

One of the traditional hotels, and rightly proud of its famous past guests such as Ernest Hemingway, Franz Liszt, and Oscar Wilde. This dignified hotel is an excellent base for visiting the old city and for extended shopping expeditions in the elegant Via Condotti. The hotel's conference facilities are located in the nearby 17th-century Palazzo Torlonia.
Via Bocca di Leone 14;
Tel 06 69 98 11.
www.hotelinghilterraroma.it

Navona

This small hotel situated in a 15th-century *palazzo*, just off the Corso del Rinascimento, is an ideal base from which to explore the city by day or night. The simple yet comfortable rooms are located on the first floor.

Via dei Sediari 8;
Tel 06 68 66 42 03.
www.hotelnavona.com

Portoghesi

This old house was converted into a small hotel about 150 years ago, but today it offers all the usual modern facilities. Located close to the Piazza Navona, in the very heart of the city, it is an ideal starting point for sightseeing or walks. It's worth staying here for the view from the roof terrace alone.
Via dei Portoghesi 1;
Tel 06 686 42 31.
www.hotelportoghesiroma.it

Raphael

Located just a few steps from the lively Piazza Navona, the Raphael is one of the most sophisticated hotels in the city. The charming façade is ivy-clad and the interior is decorated with numerous paintings, antiques, and sculptures. The rooms on the third floor of the hotel were designed by architect Richard Meier, using the finest materials and fitted with the latest sound systems. The restaurant offers a selection of superb dishes, served on attractive hand-painted plates, as well as a stunning view from the roof terrace.
Largo Febo 2;
Tel 06 68 28 31.
www.raphaelhotel.com

Nightlife

Gilda

This large, well-known club is a meeting point for chic Romans and international VIPs alike. Here you can spot politicians, actors, film stars, and sport stars dining, danc-

ing – and perhaps even indulging in a little flirting. There are several rooms and the club is divided into a disco and a bar. You will need to be smartly dressed in order to get through the door; however, entry is sometimes by formal invitation only.
Via Mario de' Fiori 97;
Tel 06 678 48 38.
www.midra.it/website/gilda/homepage.asp

New Open Gate

Start your Roman night out here, with a cocktail or two at the bar of this popular disco.
Via San Nicola da Tolentino,
Tel 06 482 44 64;
closed Sun and July–Sept.

Supperclub

A great and really unusual club with a unique ambience, located in an ancient villa. Enjoy your nightlife ancient Roman style – eat and drink while reclining on sofas, just as they did in the days of the emperors. The music, however, is contemporary.
Via de' Nari 14;
Tel 06 68 80 72 07;
19.00–3.00, daily.
www.supperclub.com

Zest Bar

A meeting place for the beautiful people, this bar is located on the top floor of the Radisson Es Hotel, with panoramic views over the city and the nearby main station, Stazione Termini. Celebrities from Italian film and television can be spotted here, as well as those from the world of fashion. In summer, you can cool off with a quick dip in the pool on the roof terrace.
Via Filippo Turati 171;
Tel 06 44 48 41.

The Roman Forum: once a market and political focal point.

Museums, music, and drama

The Colosseum

A stay in Rome should really include a visit to the Colosseum, the largest ancient structure in the city, even if the entry charges are not cheap (combined ticket with entrance to the Palatine Hill). The site is spectacular, particularly if you decide to climb to the upper circles of the arena. It once held between 50,000 and 75,000 spectators. Rent an audio guide, or make use of a human *cicerone* (guide) – provided by the state and by private travel guide companies – to bring the history and architecture of one of Rome's major monuments to life (see p. 70).

Piazza del Colosseo;
Tel 06 39 96 77 00 or
06 700 54 69;
9.00 until 1 hour before
sunset, daily, or until 16.30
in winter.

The Roman Forum

At the time when Rome was the capital of the world, the Forum Romanum, with its squares and buildings, was considered the "navel of the world". Before walking around the extensive ruins, climb the south side of the Capitoline Hill from where you can get a wonderful overview of the whole complex. The main entrances are at Piazza Santa Maria Nova near the Colosseum and the Largo Romolo e Remo. Avoid midday during high summer when the site bakes in the hot sun (see p. 64).

Tel 06 699 01 10 or
06 39 96 77 00;
9.00 until 1 hour before
sunset, daily.

Festivals and events

Caracalla's Baths

On warm summer nights the *caldarium* becomes an open-air stage for opera performances by the Teatro dell'Opera. Opera connoisseurs may find fault with the acoustics, but as a unique experience, when beautiful music fills the night sky in a magical ancient setting, it cannot be faulted (see p. 152).

Via delle Terme di Caracalla;
Tel 06 361 10 64 or
06 48 16 01;
late June–Aug.
www.operaroma.it

Easter

On Good Friday, the ceremonial *Via Crucis* (Way of the Cross) procession by torchlight, led by the pope, winds its way around the Colosseum, passing through the 14 Stations of the Cross established by Pope Benedict XIV in 1749. The procession is a reminder of Christ's last walk to Golgotha.

Estate Romana

In the summer months, Rome becomes a spectacular setting for a variety of events held in its squares, palaces, villas, gardens, and parks – from concerts, and cabarets, to drama and cinema. The city's monuments are illuminated atmospherically and musicians and entertainers perform in the streets, alleys, and squares, when the whole of the old city is transformed into an open-air stage.

Information and schedule:
Tel 06 497 11;
mid June–end Sept.
www.romaturismo.com,
www.estateromana.
comune.roma.it

Notte Bianca

Rome's White Night, when various cultural activities take place throughout the night, occurs in early September. Museums, galleries, and some public buildings can be visited free of charge. Concerts are held in locations throughout the city, and many cafés and bars remain open all night. It's a cultural experience that is free for everyone – Romans and visitors alike.

early Sept.
www.lanottebianca.it

Sport and leisure

Maratona

Like many other cities, Rome also stages a marathon. The participants are challenged to a gruelling 42.195-km (26.2-mile) race around the city, which takes in a little sightseeing en route as the runners pass the Colosseum and St Peter's, to cheering crowds and the occasional blessing from a priest.

late March.
www.maratonadiroma.it

Shopping

Alberta Gloves

While gloves are worn less these days as a simple fashion accessory, they remain a necessity in colder climates in winter. This shop carries numerous styles in every size and material, and for every conceivable occasion, with the exception of gloves required for manual work. Braces are sold here too.

Corso Vittorio Emanuele II
18; Tel 06 678 57 53.

La Chiave

Ethnic odds and ends from all over the world at low prices, and more unusual objects for the home: crockery, dream catchers, lamps, furniture, and much more.

Largo delle Stimmate 28;
Tel 06 68 30 88 48.

Rinascita

A book and record store that stocks a good selection of world music, jazz, blues, and classical recordings.

Villa delle Botteghe Oscure
5; Tel 06 69 92 24 36.

Sciù Scià Group di Biaggi Bruno

A tiny little shop selling handmade women's shoes stacked in boxes, in both classic and contemporary styles, and low- and high-heeled. Time spent rummaging here is time well spent.

Via di Torre Argentina 8;
Tel 06 68 80 67 77.

From left: Triumphal arch of Emperor Constantine I; the Via Appia Antica; the Colosseum; the Bocca della Verità – The Mouth of Truth – which is said to reveal a liar by biting off their fingers when their hand is placed in its mouth.

ANCIENT ROME

This section contains additional insider tips on places to visit, restaurants, accommodation, nightlife, and festivals and events, supplementing the information given in the "The Highlights" section (pp. 56–87).

Michelangelo's Piazza del Campidoglio on the Capitol is lined with arcades and *palazzi*.

Spazio Sette
High-quality and occasionally bizarre designer furniture and kitchen utensils fill three floors of this 17th-century *palazzo*, which has now turned into a store selling the greatest names in Italian and international design.
Via dei Barbieri 7;
Tel 06 686 97 08;
Tues–Sat 9.30–13.30, 15.30–
19.00, daily, closed Aug.

Eating and drinking

L'Insalata Ricca
How about trying something other than pasta for lunch? The salads here are refreshing, fresh, varied, and have interesting combinations, but are not too heavy on either the stomach or the wallet. If you really are in need of something a little more solid, they also have a selection of pasta, pizza, meat, and fish dishes too. One of 12 branches in this chain.
Largo dei Chiavari 85;
Tel 06 85 68 80 36;
12.00–16.00 and
19.00–24.00, daily.
www.linsalataricca.it

La Piazzetta
A pleasant gay- and lesbian-friendly restaurant, located in a little alleyway just to the north of the Colosseum. The

starters, main dishes, and desserts from the buffet are all excellent.
Vicolo del Buon Consiglio 23a; Tel 06 699 16 40;
Mon–Sat.

Quelli della Taverna
A traditional local taverna near the Teatro Argentina, serving wonderful, hearty starters and main dishes that are really simple but all the tastier for that.
Via dei Barbieri 25;
Tel 06 686 96 60.

Renato e Luisa
A modern trattoria with a penchant for French cuisine, situated near the Torre Argentina. The service can be a little indifferent, but if that doesn't put you off, you can experience some real culinary delights here.
Via dei Barbieri 25;
Tel 06 686 96 60;
Tues–Sun 8.30–24.30.
www.renatoeluisa.it

Vecchia Roma
A well-established restaurant with a terrace, frequented by high-ranking politicians and celebrities. It has been owned by the Palladino family since 1870. Vecchia Roma serves classic Italian and local Roman cuisine. The pasta, risotto, and polenta dishes,

and the diverse antipasti are always delicious.
Piazza Campitelli 18;
Tel 06 96 86 46 04;
Thurs–Tues, closed Aug.

Accommodation

Forum
A good, mid-range hotel situated behind the Imperial Forums. In fine weather, it is worth visiting the restaurant on the roof terrace, from where there is a great view.
Via Tor de' Conti 25;
Tel 06 679 24 46.
www.hotelforumrome.com

Hotel dei Gladiatori
This hotel is in an impressive position opposite the world-famous Colosseum. Although the traffic never stops, the view of the arena is fabulous, particularly from the hotel's beautiful roof terrace.
Via Labicana 125;
Tel 06 77 59 13 80.
www.hotelgladiatori.com

Nerva
An ideal base from which to explore the sites of ancient Rome, this hotel is situated close to the Roman Forum. The 19 rooms are both quiet and comfortable.
Via Tor de' Conti 3;
Tel 06 679 37 64.
www.hotelnerva.com

Perugia
A small, simple, and reliably run hotel, not far from the Colosseum. The prices are reasonable for a hotel in such a central position.
Via del Colosseo 7;
Tel 06 679 72 00.
www.hotel-perugia.
romaviva.com

Richmond
Just a few steps from the ancient monuments and the best shopping streets, this hotel is owned by the Gnecco family, who pride themselves on good service. The rooms are comfortable and there is a beautiful roof terrace, where you can breakfast in summer while enjoying the view of the Imperial Forums.
Largo Corrado Ricci 36;
Tel 06 69 94 12 56. www.
hotelrichmondroma.com

Teatro di Pompeo
A good hotel with a simple façade built on truly historic foundations: it stands on a section of the spectators' stand of the Teatro di Pompeo, the theater built by Pompey during his second consulship and opened in 55 BC. Breakfast is taken in a room with ancient Roman vaulting.
Largo del Pallaro 8;
Tel. 06 68 30 01 70. www.
hotelteatrodipompeo.it

The tomb of Pope Pius XI in St Peter's.

Museums, music, and drama

Castel Sant'Angelo
The mausoleum of Emperor Hadrian and his family, later used as a fortress and refuge by the Roman Catholic popes, has a remarkable frescoed interior and a museum displaying weapons, furniture, and objects from everyday life (see p. 106).
Lungotevere Castello 50;
Tel 06 681 91 11;
Tues–Sun 9.00–19.00.
www.castelsantangelo.com

Museo Storico Artistico Tesoro di San Pietro
The treasure chamber of St Peter's is home not only to valuable liturgical items in gold, silver, and gemstones, but also precious fragments from papal tombs and ancient sarcophagi.
St Peter's Sacristy, left-hand aisle; summer 9.00–18.00, Oct–Mar 9.00–17.00.

Festivals and events

The Easter blessing
The highpoint of the Easter celebrations in the Vatican is the *urbi et orbi* blessing ("to the city and to the world"), given by the Holy Father at midday on Easter Sunday. The blessing is given in many languages to the faithful crowds that gather in St Peter's Square from all parts of the world, and is broadcast on television to viewers on every continent.
St Peter's Square;
Easter Sunday.

Shopping

Angelo di Nepi
Italian designer fashion meets Bollywood: Nepi links two completely different worlds of fashion and uses the finest fabrics and elaborate embroidery to make his creations, which have a hint of the exotic.
Via Cola di Rienzo 267 a;
Tel 06 322 48 00.
www.angelodinepi.it

Castroni
If you tire of the traditional Italian fare such as prosciutto and pasta, espresso and grappa, this delicatessen stocks international ingredients galore, which are not available almost anywhere else in Rome – from corned beef, to hundreds of different varieties of teas. There's also an amazing selection of sweets.
Via Cola di Rienzo 196;
Tel 06 687 43 83;
Mon–Sat 8.00–20.00.
www.castroni.com

Doctor Music
A charming little music store, which stocks a good selection of new and used recordings of rock and pop, country rock, blues, and most notably, jazz on both CD and vinyl.
Via dei Gracchi 41/43;
Tel 06 320 05 43; Mon–Sat 9.30–13.00 and 16.00–20.00.

Enoteca Costantini
A cozy and richly stocked wine cellar located opposite the Castel Sant'Angelo. You'll find more than 4,000 wines on offer here, arranged clearly by region, along with around 1,000 spirits and liqueurs.
Piazza Cavour 16;
Tel 06 320 35 75;
Mon 16.30–20.00, Tues–Sat 9.00–13.00 and 16.30–20.00.
www.pierocostantini.it

Euroclero
This shop sells the garments worn by Roman Catholic men and women in their religious roles – from the simple habits for monks and nuns, to the more elaborate cassocks and vestments for priests, and not forgetting a good selection of "chaste" underwear. Candles and some rather kitsch holy figures and images are also available.
Via Paolo VI 31;
Tel 06 68 80 17 22;
Mon–Fri 9.00–13.00 and 14.00–18.00, Sat 9.00–12.30.
www.euroclero.it

Franchi
Another *alimentari* (delicatessen) worth a recommendation, with an outstanding range of italian cheeses, wines, hams, and salamis. Their ready-made snacks are also excellent.
Via Cola di Rienzo 200–204;
Tel 06 686 45 76.

Mercato della Piazza dell'Unità
A busy market hall located in the middle of the Prati district that sells everyday food as well as fine culinary treats. Cut flowers are also available.
Via Cola di Rienzo;
Mon–Sat 7.00–20.00.

Eating and drinking

Benito e Gilberto al Falco
A tiny restaurant that has been specializing in fish dishes for more than three decades, and can claim some very famous customers. Fish and seafood, freshly caught or harvested, are prepared simply and are always delicious. The wine list is extensive and the homemade desserts also come highly recommended.
Via del Falco 19;
Tel 06 686 77 69;
Tues–Sat 12.30–15.00 and 19.45–23.30.
www.dabenitoegilberto.com

Del Frate
An elegant wine bar, housed in brick vaults formerly used for storing wine. An ideal place in which to relax and satisfy any hunger pangs after a visit to the Vatican – serving some unusual dishes at reasonable prices.
Via degli Scipioni 118;
Tel 06 323 64 37;
Mon–Sat 13.00–15.00 and 19.30–1.00, Sun 19.30–1.00, closed for two weeks in Aug.

Dino & Tony
An original, convivial Roman trattoria, with bright checkered tablecloths, giant portions, singing, cheery waiters, and even a few tables outside on the (not particularly invit-

From left: View of St Peter's at night; the interior of the basilica; the ceiling of the Sistine Chapel; the Ponte Sant'Angelo, which leads over the Tiber to the Castel Sant'Angelo.

THE VATICAN

This section contains additional insider tips on places to visit, restaurants, accommodation, nightlife, and festivals and events, supplementing the information given in the "The Highlights" section (pp. 88–113).

ing) street. The antipasti alone are worth the visit.
Via Leone IV 60;
Tel 06 39 73 32 84;
Mon–Sat 12.30–15.30 and
from 19.30.

Faggiani
The Faggiani Bar is certainly worth a visit for Italian snacks and a great breakfast if you're in the location. There's a good mix of people among the clientele. The cake shop next door is really something special, where you can get the best bread, cakes, and pastries in the whole city.
Via Giuseppe Ferrari 23;
Tel 06 39 73 97 42.

Gelateria Old Bridge
Without doubt, one of the best ice-cream shops (some would say *the* best) in Rome, and generally packed with people on sunny days. The portions are usually quite generous.
Via dei Bastioni di
Michelangelo 5;
Tel 06 39 72 30 26.

Girarrosto Toscano
Tuscan cuisine in Rome? The traditional rivalries between the northern Italians and those living in the capital go back many centuries, but the contrast works really well in this restaurant. Try the home-made pasta and the delicious meat dishes.
Via Germanico 56;
Tel 06 39 72 57 17;
Tues–Sun 12.30–15.00,
20.00–23.30, closed Mon
and three weeks in Aug.

Il Simposio di Costantini
This restaurant serves a wide range of wines from Enoteca Costantini, accompanied by light or more substantial hot

dishes. Or you can just order tasty nibbles such as cheese and salami in the wine bar.
Piazza Cavour 16;
Tel 06 320 35 75;
Restaurant: Mon–Sat 12.30–
15.00 and 19.30–23.00;
Wine bar: Mon–Sat 12.30–
15.00 and 18.00–23.00.
www.pierocostantini.it

Latteria di Borgo Pio
A traditional ice-cream parlour and coffee shop with classic marble counters and tiled floor, which will transport you back to the swinging 1960s.
Via Borgo Pio 48;
Tel 06 68 80 39 55;
Mon–Sat 9.00–21.00,
closed Aug.

Osteria dell'Angelo
This restaurant is a little way north of the Vatican, but is well worth a visit for its outstanding no-nonsense, traditional cuisine. The fixed-price menus are particularly recommended and are surprisingly good value. Word has got out, so it would be a good idea to make a reservation.
Via Giovanni Bettolo 24/26;
Tel. 06 372 94 70;
Tues, Fri 13.00–14.30,
Mon–Sat 20.00–22.30.

Shanti
A popular and prettily decorated restaurant serving mildly spiced Pakistani and Indian dishes. Ideal when you need a change from pasta and pizzas.
Via Fabio Massimo 68;
Tel 06 324 49 22.

Accommodation

Monasteries and convents
Many visitors to Rome take advantage of the simple,

Prayers in church – the highpoint of every pilgrimage.

peaceful, and economic overnight accommodation in one of the many monasteries and convents located throughout the city, though most operate a strict curfew at night. Santa Susanna is the American Catholic Church in Rome and its website includes a list of convents that welcome guests.
www.santasusanna.org/
comingToRome/convents.
html#R-vatican

Columbus
The Columbus is an ideal base for prospective visitors to the Vatican, with a view of St Peter's Basilica from one end of the Via della Conciliazone. Built as a palace, the building dates from the 16th century and, in keeping with its original role, it still retains a dignified air of aristocratic charm.
Via della Conciliazone 33;
Tel 06 686 54 35.
www.hotelcolumbus.net

Farnese
A beautiful villa in the Prati quarter, which has been transformed into a quiet hotel, ideally situated within easy walking distance of the Vatican.
Via A. Farnese 30;
Tel 06 321 25 53.
www.hotelfarnese.com

Residenza Paolo VI
The Residenza Paolo VI opened as a hotel in 2000 on the former site of an Augustinian monastery. This four-star hotel has a unique location, directly on St Peter's Square, with excellent views from the terrace while sipping an aperitif.
Via Paolo VI 29;
Tel 06 68 40 39 60.
www.residenzapaolovi.com

Nightlife

Alexanderplatz Jazz Club
One of the oldest and most famous jazz clubs in Rome, Alexanderplatz plays host to both local and international musicians. There's also a bar and restaurant.
Via Ostia 9;
Tel 06 39 74 21 71;
from 20.00, concerts: from
22.00.
www.alexanderplatz.it

Fonclea
Live music has been played in this club in the Prati district for more than 30 years – from jazz, soul, and funk, to blues and rock – and entrance is free. With restaurant and pub.
Via Crescenzio 82 a;
Tel 06 689 63 02;
9.00–2.00, concerts: from
21.30.
www.fonclea.it

Museums, music, and drama

Accademia Nazionale di Santa Cecilia
Established by a group of musicians in the 16th century, this academy and music conservatory has a renowned symphony orchestra and is one of the oldest music institutions in the world.
Viale Pietro de Coubertin 34; Tel 06 80 820 58. www.santacecilia.it

Auditorium Parco della Musica
An architecturally spectacular auditorium, with three concert halls, the Parco della Musica is the largest venue of its kind in the city. One of its halls, the Sala Santa Cecilia, is said to be the largest concert hall in Europe.
Viale Pietro de Coubertin; Tel 06 80 24 12 81; 10.00–20.00, daily, guided tours on Sat, Sun, and public holidays 10.30–17.30. www.auditorium.com

Galleria Nazionale d'Arte Moderna e Contemporanea
The collection moved to its present location in 1915; it features paintings and sculpture from the 19th and 20th centuries, with a focus on Italian art.
Viale delle Belle Arti 131; Tel 06 32 29 82 21; Tues–Sun 09.00–19.00. www.gnam.beniculturali.it

Museo Nazionale degli Strumenti Musicali
This specialist museum, with over 3,000 exhibits, gives an overview of the history and development of musical instruments.
Piazza Santa Croce in Gerusalemme 9 a; Tel 06 328 10; Tues–Sun 8.30–19.30. www.museostrumentimusicali.it

Villa Torlonia
Built between 1806 and 1829, the Villa Torlonia was once the private residence of "il duce", Benito Mussolini. A number of buildings in the park are open to the public, exhibiting modern art and a collection of stained glass.
Via Nomentana 70; Tel 06 06 08; Tues–Sun 9.00–19.00. www.museivillatorlonia.it

Festivals and events

Gay Village
As part of the events of the Estate Romana, Rome's summer festival, there are celebrations in various locations in the EUR district.
EUR, June–Sept. www.gayvillage.it

Villa Celimontana Jazz Festival
Experience a wide range of jazz styles in the gardens of the Villa Celimontana on summer evenings.
Villa Celimontana; June–Aug. www.trovaromaonline.it, www.villacelimontanajazz.com

Sport and leisure

Acquasanta
Keep up your golf game, even while on vacation – this elegant 18-hole course is situated between the Via Appia Nuova and Via Appia Antica. The course is quite challenging and has fabulous views of the Colli Albani and the aqueduct of Emperor Claudius.
Via Appia Nuova 716; Tel 06 780 34 07. www.golfroma.it

Bioparco
Situated in the extensive park of the Villa Borghese, Rome's zoo houses its animals in conditions that correspond to their natural environments as closely as possible. It is actively involved in scientific and conservation education research.
Piazzale del Giardino Zoologico (Villa Borghese); Oct–Mar 9.30–17.00, Apr–Oct 9.30–18.00. www.bioparco.it

Campionati Ippico Internazionale
The park of the Villa Borghese provides a fitting location for this major equestrian sporting event, which attracts enthusiasts from all over the world. The competitions take place on the Piazza di Siena, surrounded by pine trees.
Tel 06 36 85 84 94 and 06 568 37 12; May. www.piazzadisiena.com

Cinecittà
Notable Italian directors such as Fellini, Pasolini, and Visconti shot some of their most famous films at these Roman film production studios (see p. 136).
Via Tuscolana 1055; Tel 06 72 29 32 07. www.cinecitta.com

Luneur
Recently renovated, the Luneur amusement park has been part of the EUR district for some 50 years; unlike most Italian amusement parks it has a pleasantly nostalgic atmosphere with a traditional Ferris wheel.
Via delle Tre Fontane; Tel 06 591 44 01; June–Sept. Mon– Fri 15.00–24.00, Sat, Sun 11.00–24.00. www.luneur.it

Teatro Mongiovino
A puppet show in Rome's EUR district; it also presents shows that incorporate live actors, music, and video. The Marionette Museum next to the Teatro Mongiovino has over 400 puppets.
EUR, Via Giovanni Genocchi 15; Tel 06 513 94 05.

Open-air cinema
A fabulous summer experience – watch a film under the stars on a warm evening with a gentle breeze wafting across the island in the Tiber, Isola Tiberina.
mid June–mid Sept. www.isoladelcinema.com

Stadio Olimpico
The Olympic stadium is where Serie A (the elite Italian league) football matches are held. Romans are real football enthusiasts, particularly when there's one of the infamous local derbies between S.S. Lazio and AS Roma.
Ticket sales: AS Roma: Tel 06 50 19 11; www.asroma.it Lazio: Tel 06 32 37 33; www.sslazio.it

Swimming in the Olympic pool
When Romans feel like a swim, they usually go to the beach, principally to the Lido di Ostia, but in the EUR district, you can cool off and get some exercise in the Piscina delle Rose.
EUR, Viale America 20; mid-June–mid-Sept 9.00–18.00.

From left: Evening atmosphere across the Tiber; a street scene in Trastevere; graffiti adorns the walls of the Ex Mattatoio in Testaccio; the caryatids at the magnificent Villa Giulia.

FURTHER AFIELD

This section contains additional insider tips on places to visit, restaurants, accommodation, nightlife, and festivals and events, supplementing the information given in the "The Highlights" section (pp. 114–137).

Spas

Hammam la culla del benessere
Relax after a tiring day's sightseeing and recuperate at these beautiful Turkish baths.
Via della Maratona 87;
Tel 06 36 29 85 73;
Tues–Sun 12.00–21.00.
www.hammamroma.it

Sporting Palace
Massages, a range of body treatments, and the standard fitness and cardio equipment are available here. There are also solaria, a large swimming pool, and a hair salon.
Via Carlo Sigonio 21 a;
Tel 06 788 79 18;
Mon–Fri 9.30–22.30,
Sat 9.30–20.00.
www.sporting-palace.com

Shopping

Mercatino di Ponte Milvio
Antiques, furniture, and crafts are traded at this market, not far from the Olympic stadium. Some of the stalls are positioned beside the Tiber.
Lungotevere Coparati;
1st weekend of every month (Sat 15.00–19.00, Sun 8.00–19.00).

Mercato dell'Antiquariato di Piazza Verdi
A flea market in the Villa Borghese area, with antiques, furniture, objets d'art, and reproductions.
Piazza Giuseppe Verdi;
4th Sunday of every month, 9.00–20.00.

Mercato di Testaccio
A covered market, much loved by locals. The fruit and vegetable stands are a treat for the eyes as well as for the taste buds, and you can also

buy shoes, many of them good quality and good value for money.
Piazza Testaccio;
Mon–Sat 7.30–13.30.

Volpetti
A delicatessen that is well known throughout Rome; its olive oils, hams, and cheeses are highly recommended. The Volpettis have been scouring the country for decades, searching for new delicacies for their range.
Via Marmorata 47;
Tel 06 574 23 52;
Mon–Sat 8.00–14.00, Mon, Wed–Sat 17.00–20.15.
www.volpetti.com

Eating and drinking

Arancia Blu
Relatively inexpensive vegetarian restaurant in the San Lorenzo quarter, with unusual and tasty dishes made from fresh ingredients. We recommend the great selection of chocolate waffles for dessert.
Via dei Latini 55;
Tel 06 445 41 05.
www.sanlorenzoroma.org

Delizie di pizze
Although relatively new, the Delizie di pizze has already acquired an excellent reputation and some of the pizzas made here are said to be the best in the city.
Via Simeto 8–10; 8.00–15.00 and 16.30–21.00, daily.

La Pergola
An award-winning restaurant in the Cavalieri Hilton Hotel. Many Romans regard this as the best gourmet restaurant in Rome.
Via Alberto Cadlolo 101;
Tel 06 35 09 21 52.
www.cavalieri-hilton.it

Pommidoro
An excellent pizzeria with a good atmosphere, away from the standard tourist routes, in the San Lorenzo quarter.
Piazza dei Sanniti 44;
Tel 06 445 26 92; Mon–Sat 12.00–16.00, 20.00–24.00.

Accommodation

Casa Internazionale delle Donne
This women-only hotel is based in a 17th-century convent. The rooms are simple, many overlooking the magnolia tree in the inner courtyard.
Via S. Francesco di Sales 1a;
Tel 06 68 40 17 24.
www.casainternazionaledelledonne.org

Cavalieri Hilton
This large luxury hotel, part of the Hilton chain, is situated on the Monte Mario. The panoramic view over Rome is quite breathtaking.
Via Alberto Cadlolo 101;
Tel 06 350 91.
www.cavalieri-hilton.it

Hotel Art by the Spanish Steps
This chic designer hotel is located in the picturesque, cobbled artists' district of Via Margutta. With its clever use of lighting and distinct mix of antique and modern furniture, it creates a special atmosphere for its guests.
Via Margutta 56; Tel 06 32 87 11. www.hotelart.it

Lord Byron
A small hotel with all the comfort of a luxury one, in the quiet and charming vicinity of the Villa Borghese.
Via Giuseppe de Notaris 5;
Tel 06 322 45 41.
www.lordbyronhotel.com

Radisson SAS
Close to the main Termini station, the Radisson offers individually designed rooms with every comfort. The hotel has two restaurants, and a swimming pool on the roof terrace.
Via Filippo Turati 171;
Tel 06 44 48 41.
www.radisson.com/romeit

Sant'Anselmo
Situated on the Aventine Hill, the Sant'Anselmo hotel lies in a small park with beautiful orange trees and is an oasis of calm, away from the hectic life of the city.
Piazza di Sant'Anselmo 2;
Tel 06 57 00 57.
www.aventinohotels.com

Trastevere
This small, inexpensive hotel makes an ideal base for an evening expedition through Trastevere. Families with children, or small groups, can rent one of the apartments.
Via Luciano Manara 24;
Tel 06 581 47 13.
www.hoteltrastevere.net

Nightlife

Big Mama
A long-established live music club located in Trastevere. Blues, jazz, and rock musicians have been appearing here since 1984.
Vicolo San Francesco a Ripa 18; Tel 06 581 25 51; 21.00–1.30, daily, shows from 22.30. www.bigmama.it

Goa
A club in the Ostiense quarter that features international DJs and also plays what's hot in Goa, India.
Via Giuseppe Libetta 13;
Tel 06 574 82 77,
Tues–Sun 23.00–4.00.

The beach at Ostia, before the crowds arrive.

Museums, music, and drama

Cerveteri

This town was once an important Etruscan city-state. It is now famous for several ancient necropolises, the highlight of which is the Necropoli della Banditaccia, located north-west of the town. This large tomb complex contains numerous graves from the Etruscan civilization (see p. 146).
Necropoli della Banditaccia; Tel 06 994 00 01; Tues–Sun 8.30 until sunset.

Museo Nazionale di Cerveteri

A 15th-century *palazzo* situated in the heart of the medieval town displays the art treasures that were discovered in the Etruscan graves found under the cliffs of Cerveteri and in the surrounding area. The finds from the necropolises date from the 9th to the 1st centuries BC, and they document the long history of this ancient settlement. There are fascinating decorative bronze vessels from the Sorbo necropolis, as well as the Corinthian and Attic ceramics, principally vases, found in the necropolis of Monte Abatone (see p. 146).

Piazza Santa Maria; Tel 06 994 13 54; Tues–Sun 8.30–18.30.

Frascati

Famous for its wine, the town of Frascati, down river from ancient Tusculum, has numerous grand villas from the Renaissance period. One of the villas, built for a Roman noble, is the 17th-century Villa Aldobrandini; set within a large park (see p. 148).
Via Cardinal Massaia 112, Frascati; Tel 06 942 93 31; (tickets available from the tourist office for the Villa Aldobrandini gardens).

Ostia Antica

Many ancient sites have been successively built over at different times in the past, but this is not the case with Ostia Antica. Rome's former port is therefore exceptionally well preserved and today provides a fascinating glimpse into the lives of the ancient Romans. Visitors can see villas belonging to high-ranking patricians, multi-level tenements, baths, arenas, studios, and shops, as well as public toilets!
Scavi di Ostia, Viale dei Romagnoli 717, Ostia; Tel 06 56 35 80 99; Tues–Sun 8.30–16.00 winter, 8.30–18.00 summer.

Museo Nazionale di Tarquinia

This collection is housed in the 15th-century Palazzo Vitelleschi. All the archeological finds come from Latium (known as the cradle of the Roman Empire and part of modern-day Lazio); they show how the Etruscans portrayed life after death. Some particularly fine examples are the painted friezes and a terracotta frieze with winged horses; there are also sarcophagi, amphorae, utensils, and jewelry. One of the highlights is the portrait of a woman giving a greyhound a drink (see p. 146).
Piazza Cavour, Tarquinia; Tel 0766 85 60 36; Tues–Sun 8.30–19.30.

Villa Adriana

The former summer residence of the Emperor Hadrian covers a site of about 120 hectares (296 acres) and contains many reminders of the emperor's extensive travels through the provinces of the Roman Empire. Later used as a source of stone for building, the site is now a collection of ruins but is still imposing and impressive (see p. 144).
via Villa Adriana 204, Tivoli; 9.00 until 1 hour before sunset, daily.
www.villa-adriana.net

Villa d'Este

The villa was built for Cardinal Ippolito d'Este between 1550 and 1572. A large-scale Renaissance building in the old medieval city of Tivoli, it is mainly visited for its garden, which makes elaborate use of water with fountains, cascades, and pools. It was the model for many later European gardens (see p. 144).

Piazza Trento, Tivoli; Tues–Sun 8.30 until 2 hours before sunset.
www.villadestetivoli.info

Festivals and events

Cosmophonies

The ancient Roman arena located in Ostia Antica forms an atmospheric backdrop for open-air music concerts and performances of drama and dance during the summer months.
Tel 06 565 71 49; June and July.
www.cosmophonies.com

Tivoli

The town plays host to a number of special festivals and events each year, including a procession bearing an image of the Madonna through the streets to the cathedral, which takes place on the first Sunday in May. There is also a mass and procession with events and dancing to celebrate the day of St Lawrence, the town's patron saint on 10 August, and a festival celebrating the grape harvest with floats and wine tasting, 10–30 September.
www.tibursuperbum.it/engl/

Sport and leisure

Aquafelix Parco Acquatico

A water park located near Civitavecchia, a sea port some 80 km (50 miles) north-west of Rome.
www.aquafelix.it

Aquapiper

Splash, slide, and swim to your heart's content in this beautifully designed water park close to Guidonia, to the north-east of Rome.
www.aquapiper.it

From left: Promenade by the sea – the Lido di Ostia; fountains play at the Villa d'Este in Tivoli; Villa Aldobrandini in Frascati; a view of Castel Gandolfo, the pope's summer residence.

BEYOND ROME

This section contains additional insider tips on places to visit, restaurants, accommodation, nightlife, and festivals and events, supplementing the information given in the "The Highlights" section (pp. 138–149).

Bagni di Tivoli

These thermal baths have been in constant use since ancient times. The "white waters" come from a spring fed by Lago Regina and Lago Colonelle, and are warmer than room temperature all year round. The whiteness of the water is due to the wealth of minerals it contains. The mineral water has an antibacterial effect and also helps ease inflammation of the skin (see p. 144).
Acque Albule, Via M. Nicodemi 9, Tivoli; Tel 0774 354.

Castel Fusano Nature Reserve

A nature reserve located near modern Ostia, where you can lie in the sun, swim in the sea, and enjoy the beautiful natural surroundings. The beach is a good 5 km (3 miles) long so there is room for everyone to sunbathe and play sport if they wish.

Lago di Bolsena

Venture out of Rome for the day and visit this beautiful freshwater crater lake where you can swim. It is a 100-km (62-mile) drive via Viterbo, taking the SS 20 to the north-west of Rome.
Tourist Office, Piazza Matteotti, Bolsena; Tel 0761 77 99 23. www.comunebolsena.it

Parco dei Mostri, Bomarzo

The "Park of Monsters" is some 90 km (56 miles) north of Rome; it is advisable to check opening times before setting off. Set amid thick vegetation, large, grotesque statues are carved out of boulders. There's also a

restaurant and children's playground.
Tel 0761 92 40 29; from 8.00 until sunset, daily. www.parcodeimostri.com

Zoomarine Italia, Torvaianica

An entertainment park for adults and children alike that primarily concentrates on marine animals, but also has a tropical bird forest. There are activities such as wild-water rides but the emphasis is on promoting respect for nature and the protection of the environment. It is located near Pomezia, south of Rome.
Tel 06 91 53 40 01; July to mid-Sept daily, Apr–June closed Mon, low season Sat/Sun only. Check website before you go. www.zoomarine.it

Eating and drinking

Adriano, Tivoli

The Hotel Adriano is an ideal place to stay when visiting the Villa Adriana. The restaurant has elegant rooms and a shaded terrace. The cuisine is outstanding and the hotel has played host to many prominent guests, including Queen Elizabeth II, Jacqueline Kennedy, Liv Ullmann, and Federico Fellini.
Largo Yourcenar 2; Tel 0774 38 22 35. www.hoteladriano.it

Accommodation

Aran Blu Hotel, Lido di Ostia

A modern four-star hotel with a steel and glass façade, overlooking the beach and opposite the port. Inside, the Art Caffè is decorated with contemporary art. The hotel also

has a terrace bar, restaurant, and a fitness suite.
Lungomare Duca degli Abruzzi 72, Tel. 06 56 34 02 25. www.aranhotels.com

Courtyard Rome Airport, Fiumicino Rome

With 187 comfortable, modern rooms, this four-star hotel is convenient for visitors arriving in Rome by plane in need of overnight accommodation nearby. There is an in-house restaurant, "The Glass", and an outdoor pool that can be used during the summer months.
Via Portuense 2470; Tel 06 99 93 51. www.marriott.com

San Marco, Tarquinia

This hotel is on the same square as the Museo Nazionale di Tarquinia. The restaurant offers typical regional dishes, some prepared to historical recipes. The American bar stocks over 100 cocktails, whiskeys, and rums.
Piazza Cavour 18; Tel 0766 84 22 34. www.san-marco.com

Castello della Castelluccia

The romantic Castello della Castelluccia was built in the 12th and 13th centuries. Situated north-west of Rome and outside the major ring road, this hotel is far removed from the hustle and bustle of the metropolis. It offers a romantic atmosphere and the finest service. Spoil yourself in the restaurant, enjoy the pool and spa facilities, or play a round of golf at the nearby course.
Via Carlo Cavina; Tel 06 30 20 70 41. www.lacastelluccia.com

La Posta Vecchia

One of the best hotels in the world, according to the trade press. Located on the coast at Ladispoli, this upmarket hotel offers pure luxury and every imaginable service. The 19 rooms and suites are expensively fitted out in keeping with the 17th-century villa in which they are housed – guests are surrounded by valuable antiques. Before it was turned into a luxury hotel, the villa was the home of John Paul Getty, who restored the building at great expense. Hotel guests can visit the in-house museum at any time; non-residents must apply in advance.
Palo Laziale; Tel 06 994 95 01. www.lapostavecchia.com

Residenza D'Epoca Rodrigo de Vivar, Ostia Antica

Relax in the country in a cozy, rustic ambience. The staff are friendly and the hotel's restaurant serves traditional Roman cuisine. In terms of transport, the hotel is conveniently placed: just a few minutes from Fiumicino airport, not far from the beach – and when the traffic is quiet, you can be in the heart of Rome in around 30 minutes.
Piazza della Rocca 18, Ostia Antica; Tel 07 58 15 51 24.

Camping, Villagio Flaminio

Located a good 6 km (4 miles) north of the city, this campsite, which also has small chalets to rent and a swimming pool, is a useful alternative to overnight accommodation in city hotels, particularly in terms of cost.
Via Flaminia Nuova 821; Tel 06 333 26 04; all year round, except Jan–Feb.

MAJOR MUSEUMS

Rome is not just extremely rich in monuments, but also boasts a wealth of cultural heritage. When deciding which of Rome's museums to visit first, the Vatican Museums are usually top of the list for most visitors, which unfortunately results in long queues at the entrance. Other outstanding collections include the small but exquisite Galleria Borghese; the national collection of paintings in the Palazzo Barberini; and the Museo Nazionale Romano, one of the largest archeological museums in the world. The Capitoline Museums, the oldest public collection of art and antiques in the world, are particularly noteworthy in a city that is full of museums, and house a collection whose richness can only be hinted at in these pages.

The Vatican City lies behind the imposing 15-m (49-feet) high colonnades of St Peter's Square (right). The area open to the public includes the museum collections, which are housed in rooms in the former papal palace converted to display exhibits. Far right: On entering the museum complex, the visitor is greeted by an impressive spiral ramp.

INFO
*The Vatican Museums,
Viale Vaticano;
Tel 06 69 88 49 47;
April–Oct Mon–Sat
8.45–16.45, Nov–Mar
8.45–13.45; Metro A
Cipro-Musei Vaticani.*

The Sistine Chapel

The Sistine Chapel (named after Pope Sixtus IV) is famous for its ceiling, commissioned by Pope Julius II and painted by Michelangelo between 1508 and 1512; it immediately established the sculptor's name as a painter. Since their restoration at the end of the 1980s, the scenes on the ceiling, ranging from the *Creation of the World* to the *Drunkenness of Noah*, are vibrant and vivid once more. The scenes were painted over the old flattened barrel-vault ceiling, which had been a bright blue with

Simply breathtaking: Michelangelo's ceiling in the Sistine Chapel.

gold stars. The frescoes on the walls of the chapel are by notable 15th-century artists including Perugino, Ghirlandaio, and Botticelli (see p. 100).

In addition to the later museum buildings, the Vatican collections are housed in rooms in the papal palace. Most of the building that we see today dates back to the Renaissance popes Nicholas V, Alexander VI, and Julius II. Among the architects employed to work on the palace were Donato Bramante, Baldassare Peruzzi, Giulio Romano, and Jacopo and Andrea Sansovino.

The history of the collection

The collection was founded by Pope Julius II (1503–13) with notable ancient pieces such as *Apollo Belvedere*, the *Laocoön* from the Domus Aurea of Emperor Nero, the *Antinous Belveder*, and the *Belvedere Torso*. During German historian Johann Joachim Winckelmann's management of the papal collections (from 1763), additional works of art and other collections were added to the already extensive list of treasures. Many of the rooms in the palace were converted into display areas under Pope Clement XIV (1769–74), and the museum space was further extended during the centuries that followed. The popes were among the first rulers to open their art collections to the public, promoting knowledge of art history and culture.

There are four separate collections: Egyptian, Etruscan, Greco-Roman, and Christian-Western art, with additional rooms with further exhibits in the Vatican palaces. Thanks to a number of donations, there are also several individual museums of note.

Egyptian Museum

Founded under Pope Gregory XVI in 1839, the Museo Gregoriano Egizio exhibits Egyptian antiquities including mummies, sarcophagi, statues, monuments, and rolls of papyrus. Many of the exhibits were brought into Italy through trade or as gifts in ancient times, and were discovered in and around Rome.

Impressive mosaics and sculptures in the Sala Rotonda in the Museo Pio-Clementino.

THE VATICAN MUSEUMS

With more than 50,000 exhibits, the Vatican Museums, comprising a series of individual collections, form the largest self-contained museum complex in the world. The longest of the four tours suggested guides the visitor around a route of 7 km (over 4 miles). Built up over four centuries by the popes, the museums' collections form a superlative overview of art dating from antiquity and the Renaissance (see p. 102).

Giotto's *Stefaneschi* triptych (around 1300), in the Pinacoteca.

Etruscan Museum

The treasures of the Museo Gregoriano Etrusco offer an insight into the Etruscans who ruled central Italy before the great Roman Empire, and demonstrate the richness of their culture. The collection includes tombs from the necropolises of Cerveteri, as well as jewelry, bronzes, ceramics, vessels, weapons, tools, chariots, and the remarkable statue *Mars of Todi.*

Classical antiquities

The collection of Greek and Roman statues, reliefs, vases, and wall paintings are principally displayed in the Museo Chiaramonti, the Museo Pio-Clementino, in the Braccio Nuovo, and in the Museo Gregoriano Profano.
In addition to the many portrait busts and statues of emperors and philosophers, the famous works collected by Julius II already mentioned are worth particular attention. Roman copies of Greek masterpieces such as *Apoxyomenos* (*The Scraper*) by Lysippus, the *Cnidian Venus* and the *Apollo Sauroktonos* by Praxiteles are impressive – as are the *Doryphoros* (*The Spear Bearer*) and the *Wounded Amazon* by Polyclitus, the Greek *Three Graces* and the *Athena and Marsyas* by Myron (original, after 450 BC). Original Roman works of note include the statue of *Augustus of Prima-*

porta and the fresco of the *Aldobrandini Wedding.*

Christian-Western art

The Museo Pio Cristiano and the Vatican library, designed by Domenico Fontana in 1587, exhibit a collection of relics, liturgical objects, and small precious items made from materials such as ivory, glass, metal, and textiles, many dating back to the early Christian period. The inspiring *Perseus with the Head of Medusa*, a masterpiece of classicism by Antonio Canova (1800), is on display in the Cortile del Belvedere.

Vatican palaces

The Appartamento Borgia of Pope Alexander VI contains six rooms decorated with fine frescoes by Pinturicchio and artists from his studio between 1492 and 1495; modern religious art is also on display here.
The loggias and the three *Stanze di Raffaeollo* ("Raphael's rooms") are especially worth seeing. The latter, dating from the early 16th century, represent one of the pinnacles of Renaissance painting: the *Stanza della Segnatura* contains one of Raphael's best-known works, *The School of Athens*, which depicts philosophers and scientists from ancient times, and the *Dispùta del Sacramento* portraying images of the saints; the other *stanze* include the beautiful frescoes *Fire in the Borgo* and the *Expulsion of Heliodorus from the Temple.*
The chapel of Pope Nicholas V was decorated in around 1455 by Fra Angelico with scenes from the lives of St Laurence and St Stephen. The Sistine Chapel (small image, p. 166 left), constructed between 1473 and 1484, is home to Michelangelo's world-famous masterpiece, depicting scenes from the story of the creation on the chapel's ceiling and the *Last Judgement* (1534–41) on the altar wall.

Guido Reni painted his *Crucifixion of St Peter* in 1604; now in the Pinacoteca.

Pinacoteca Vaticana

The paintings in the collection of the Pinacoteca Vaticana are arranged chronologically in a building constructed specifically for the purpose in 1932. Its main attractions include the wall tapestries originally designed by Raphael for the Sistine Chapel, the *Madonna of Foligno*, and the *Transfiguration of Christ* by the same artist. Giotto's *Stefaneschi* triptych is impressive, as is the *Deposition from the Cross* by Caravaggio; there are also very fine pieces by Leonardo da Vinci, Bellini, Titian, Paolo Veronese, Guido Reni, Murillo, and Jose de Ribera, among others.

The collection is housed in the former Villa Borghese Pinciana, a beautiful late-Renaissance residence. It was built for aristocrat and prelate Scipio Borghese as a place in which to entertain and to display his collection of works of art. With an imposing staircase leading to the entrance, superb frescoes, and ornate marble decorative detail inside, the building is a work of art in itself.

INFO
*Galleria Borghese,
Piazzale del Museo
Borghese 5;
Tel 06 841 39 79;
Tues–Sun 8.30–19.00,
Entry tickets:
Tel 06 328 10 or
www.ticketeria.it*

Apollo and Daphne

The group of *Apollo and Daphne* (1622–25), one of Bernini's major works, portrays an episode from Ovid's *Metamorphoses*. According to a legend from ancient Greek mythology, retold throughout history, the story goes that the god Apollo desired the nymph Daphne. However, she did not return his love and took flight. Apollo tried to catch her, but as he reached her she began to turn into a laurel tree to escape him, her arms becoming branches, her skin bark and her toes turning to roots.

Apollo and Daphne by Bernini (1622–25).

Bernini succeeded in producing a remarkably lifelike, dramatic sculpture, in which skin, hair, leaves, and roots are all beautifully reproduced in cold, unforgiving marble. The life-sized statue is now displayed to dramatic effect in the beauti-

The Villa Borghese was designed by architects Giovanni Vasanzio and Flaminio Ponzio for Cardinal Scipio Borghese, from the noble House of Borghese, who had acquired the land on which it was to be built – located outside the city walls and planted with vineyards – in 1605. Work on the construction of the palace began in 1612, and it was virtually completed in one year. The cardinal then had the surrounding area converted into a formal park and garden, the landscaping of which was not finished until 1620. The layout of the current park, however, dates from the 18th century, when it was converted to the English style in keeping with the tastes of the time.

The history of the collection

Scipio Caffarelli Borghese's magnificent villa on the Pincio Hill was constructed in the 17th century, but the superb interior that visitors see today, is mostly thanks to a redesign carried out in the mid-18th century. In 1807, Camillo Borghese, who was married to Napoleon Bonaparte's sister Paolina, was pressurized by the French emperor to sell the Borghese collection to France and consequently this part of the collection can today be seen in the Louvre in Paris. However, the Borghese family went on to acquire further ancient sculptures, which were also

displayed at the villa. In 1891 the family's valuable collection of paintings was added, which until then had been kept in the family's palace in Rome. In 1902, the whole villa complex passed to the Italian state and the collection was opened to the general public.

Ground floor

The rooms on the ground floor primarily contain sculptures along with some Roman floor mosaics dating from the 3rd century AD and some paintings, including works by Annibale Carracci and Guido Reni. Particularly outstanding sculptural works are the statue of Emperor Augustus in his role as supreme priest and a Roman

Paolina Borghese, Napoleon's sister, as Venus, depicted by Antonio Canova (1805–08).

GALLERIA BORGHESE

Relatively small in size, the Galleria Borghese began life as a private collection. Situated on the outskirts of the city, despite its compact size, the Galleria Borghese's superb sculptures and paintings make it one of Rome's best museums (see p. 132). The naturalistic Villa Borghese Gardens are also a popular tourist attraction.

copy of *Athena Parthenos*. The original of the latter, now lost, was made of gold and ivory and stood approximately 12 m (39 feet) in height. A religious effigy of the goddess Athena, it was created in around 440 BC for the Parthenon on the Acropolis in Athens by the Greek sculptor Phidias.

Among other highlights of the Galleria Borghese are sculptural figures by Giovanni Lorenzo Bernini, commissioned by Scipio Borghese between 1620 and 1625. These are some of the celebrated baroque sculptor and architect's early works and include *Apollo and Daphne*, *Pluto and Proserpina*, the statue of a youthful David, as well as *Aeneas, Anchises and Ascanius Fleeing Troy*.

Further works by Bernini, including the personification of *Truth*, produced in around 1655, were later additions to the collection. However, all these works show his masterly handling of marble, his wonderful use of light and shade, and the emotion that he brought to his work, so characteristic of the baroque period.

Bernini often chose to focus on pivotal moments in history, such as depicting a youthful David in the act of hurling his stone at Goliath. Full of life and movement, his work can be contrasted with the restrained classicism of Antonio Canova's masterpiece *Paolina Borghese* (1805–08), in which Canova depicts Napoleon's sister as Venus reclining on a couch. The sculpting of the folds of the fabric is particularly fine.

Upper floor

This part of the gallery is mainly devoted to the painting collection, which primarily dates from the Italian Renaissance and the baroque period. Also exhibited here are busts by Bernini, including two portraying his client Scipio Borghese, and his *bozzetto* (clay model) for an "equestrian statue of King Louis XIV of France", as well as ancient and baroque sculptures by other artists.

For examples of outstanding Renaissance art, look for pieces by Antonello da Messina, Giovanni Bellini, Lorenzo Lotto, and Paolo Veronese, and particularly Raphael's famous *Deposition* and two portraits. Also impressive are Correggio's *Danae* (c. 1531), depicting an episode from Ovid's *Metamorphoses*, and Titian's *Sacred and Profane Love* (c. 1514). A good example of the mannerist style is Agnolo Bronzino's *John the Baptist* (c. 1525).

Caravaggio's paintings are fine examples of early Roman baroque, including the *Madonna dei Palafrenieri* with Mary, the infant Jesus, and Anna, Mary's mother; the *Sick Bacchus*, a self-portrait of the artist; and *St Jerome*. Works by Domenichino, Pietro da Cortona, the German Lucas Cranach the Elder, and the Flemish baroque genius Peter Paul Rubens are also particularly impressive.

Above: the *Sick Bacchus* by Caravaggio (1594). Right: Raphael's *Deposition* (1507).

The Palazzo Barberini is a perfect example of a grand Roman house of the baroque period, and its size is equally impressive. Laid out around three sides of a forecourt, with wide arched windows, the building is typical of its period. The rich ornamentation and frescoes inside the palace are also highly characteristic.

INFO
*Palazzo Barberini,
Via delle Quattro
Fontane 13;
Palazzo Corsini, Via
della Lungara 10,
Villa Farnesina,
Via della Lungara 230,
Tel 06 48 45 91.*

An Old Testament story gets a dramatic twist

Caravaggio's depiction of the biblical scene of *Judith and Holofernes* shows Judith, who became a heroine for the people of Israel when she freed her native town of Bethulia from the Assyrians. The town was besieged and had almost run out of fresh water, when Judith crept out and made her way into the Assyrians' camp and the tent of the enemy commander Holofernes. She promised him that he would be able to capture

***Judith and Holofernes** by Caravaggio (1598).*

Bethulia, but after a feast, she cut off the drunken commander's head. Caravaggio portrays the brutality of the act of murder in his painting dating from around 1598. Famed for his realism and sense of drama, Caravaggio made use of light and dark to highlight the part of a painting to which he wanted to draw the viewer's attention.

The most important baroque palace in Rome was commissioned by Maffeo Barberini for the Baberini family – he later became Pope Urban VIII – and was designed by architects Carlo Maderno, Gianlorenzo Bernini, and Francesco Borromini. Work began on the palace in 1625. Worthy of particular attention are its two staircases: on the right, a spiral staircase in oval form by Borromini; and on the left, a rectangular staircase by Bernini. In the Gran Salone, located on the second floor, the ceiling fresco by Pietro da Cortona glorifies the Barberini dynasty. The three bees are their heraldic symbol. Other frescoes were painted by Andrea Sacchi. The Palazzo Corsini (1729–32), situated on the western side of the Tiber, can be traced back in its present form to Fernando Fuga. The Villa Farnesina (1508–11) nearby is the work of Baldassare Peruzzi; its interior contains frescoes by Raphael, Giulio Romano, Baldassare Peruzzi himself, Sebastiano del Piombo, and Sodoma.

Palazzo Barberini

The works in the collection housed in the Palazzo Barberini are displayed in chronological order, with the first floor being mainly devoted to Italian paintings from the 12th to 17th centuries, along with Flemish, French, and German paintings as well. These include such masterpieces as Raphael's portrait of *La Fornarina*. The features of the unknown sitter, who also appears in other works by Raphael, are believed to be that of the artist's great love and inspirational muse. Other highlights of the museum include Titian's *Venus and Adonis*, several *Passion* scenes by Tintoretto, as well as his *Christ and the Woman Taken in Adultery*, Caravaggio's *Judith and Holofernes* (see box left), and *Narcissus* by the same artist. The collection includes works by Renaissance artists such as Filippo Lippi, Lorenzo

***The Massacre of the Niobids**, a mythological scene by Andrea Camassei (1640).*

GALLERIA NAZIONALE D'ARTE ANTICA

The National Gallery of Ancient Art's collection of paintings, is housed across two different sites – the Palazzo Barberini and the Palazzo Corsini. The collection contains an impressive cross section of European paintings from the Middle Ages onward. A significant number of the exhibits once belonged to noble Roman families. An associated collection of graphic art is located in the Villa Farnesina.

Narcissus by Caravaggio (late 16th century).

Lotto, and Sodoma, and mannerist painters such as Agnolo Bronzino and El Greco. Another part of the collection features Roman, Neapolitan, and Bolognese baroque painting, with work by Pietro da Cortona, Giovanni Lanfranco, Luca Giordano, Mattia Preti, Guercino, Domenichino, and Guido Reni. In the Palazzo Barberini you can also see a *Portrait of King Henry VIII of England*, by court painter Hans Holbein the Younger, and the well-known *Portrait of Erasmus of Rotterdam* by Quentin Massys.

The second floor of the Palazzo Barberini is filled with paintings from the 18th century, primarily of Italian and French origin, but also featuring views of Rome by Vanvitelli and views of Venice by Canaletto. The original Appartamento Settecentesco of Cornelia Costanza Barberini, furnished between 1750 and 1770, offers a glimpse into the aristocratic life of the times, and contains furniture, porcelain, and jewelry.

Palazzo Corsini

The Palazzo Corsini mainly displays works from the Corsini family collection, which was sold to the Italian state in 1883 along with the palace itself. The collection was begun by Cardinal Neri Maria Corsini. The palace still has associations with Queen Christina of Sweden, who lived in a palace built earlier on the site from 1659 until her death in 1689. The exhibits are mainly Italian paintings from the 14th to the 17th century, encompassing religious and historical works, and landscapes. They include pieces by Fra Angelico, Annibale Carracci, Luca Giordano, Giovanni Lanfranco, Guido Reni, Carlo Maratta, and successors to Caravaggio, including Orazio Gentileschi – and also pieces by Peter Paul Rubens, Anthony van Dyck, Esteban Murillo, Jose de Ribera, and Angelica Kauffmann.

Gabinetto Nazionale delle Stampe

The national graphic art collection is housed in the Villa Farnesina and has more than 150,000 drawings and prints from the 15th to the 19th century. Built for a rich banker and the treasurer of Pope Julius II at the beginning of the 16th century, it was originally intended as a summer retreat. Acquired by the Farnese family in 1577, it is now owned by the state.

Above: *Victorian Family* by C.J. Langley (1850).
Right: *St Jean François* by Domenico Muratori (1740).

Built in the 19th century on the site of a villa belonging to Pope Sixtus V, the Palazzo Massimo alle Terme was formerly a Jesuit seminary, and was used as a military hospital in World War II. Acquired by the state in 1981, it was restored and adapted to house part of the museum's collection. It exhibits many superb ancient sculptures, including the relief of a gladiatorial battle dating from the 2nd century AD (far right).

INFO

Museo Nazionale Romano: Terme di Diocleziano with the Aula Ottagona, Palazzo Massimo alle Terme, Palazzo Altemps; Tel 06 39 96 77 00; Tues–Sun 9.00–19.45.

Hermes Ludovisi

This marble statue of Hermes, the messenger of the gods, easily recognizable by his winged helmet, is a Roman 1st-century copy of a Greek bronze original from around 440 BC attributed to Phidias. After Hellas (the ancient Greek name for Greece) was incorporated into the Roman Empire, Greek works of art were very much in vogue and were so coveted by the Romans that they had many statues brought to Rome from Greece. In order to meet the enormous demand from private clients and for public statues, many

Founded in 1889, the National Museum of Rome was initially housed in an abandoned 16th-century Carthusian monastery, which had been built over the remains of the baths of Emperor Diocletian, the largest of all the imperial Roman baths. The museum contains many sculptures, objects from everyday life in ancient Rome, and a collection of inscriptions. The Aula Ottagona (Octagonal Hall), which is also part of the baths complex, displays some of the sculpture collection, along with a collection of inscriptions and *stele* (funeral stones). The Palazzo Massimo, not far away, is home to the principal sculpture collection, and also

contains a coin collection and frescoes. The Palazzo Altemps, located north of Piazza Navona, houses the important Ludovisi and Mattei collections.

Terme di Diocleziano

Exhibits on display in the Baths of Diocletian, the museum's original site, include weapons and items from everyday life in ancient Rome, as well as statues, sarcophagi, and mosaics. In the Aula Ottagona, one of the largest domed rooms in the baths, two statues stand out among the many on display (most of which are Roman copies of Greek masterpieces): *The Athlete* and *The Boxer*. These two bronze

sculptures from the Hellenistic period are superbly sculpted with great realism – the boxer's scars and broken nose are visible.

Palazzo Massimo

Built at the end of the 19th century, the Palazzo Massimo was once part of a Jesuit college. The exhibits on display cover four floors and represent the various themes and styles prevalent in ancient Rome between the 1st and 4th centuries AD, discovered in various locations in and around the city. Among the exhibits is the Bambina di Grottarossa, the mummified body of a child discovered together with its wooden doll by workmen in 1964.

Hermes Ludovisi, a Roman copy in marble of a bronze original by Phidias (5th century BC).

pieces were copied in marble in considerable numbers. Many of the originals no longer exist, having been melted down for scrap, mainly in the Middle Ages. So it is thanks to these ancient Roman copies that we still have knowledge of the Greek masterpieces today.

A relic from a vibrant era: Roman marble sarcophagus with reliefs, around AD 100.

MUSEO NAZIONALE ROMANO

The Museo Nazionale Romano (the National Museum of Rome) is one of the largest and most important archeological museums in the world. Due to the size of the collection, it is displayed in three different buildings in separate locations: in the Palazzo Massimo, which is not far from the Aula Ottagona, part of the ancient Terme di Diocleziano (the Baths of Diocletian), and in the Palazzo Altemps (near the Piazza Navona).

Mosaics and sculptures are displayed on the ground floor, including many busts and statues of Roman emperors. The *Emperor Augustus* is depicted as Pontifex Maximus (supreme priest) with a toga drawn up over his head. Also located on the ground floor is the famous *Wounded Niobid*, a figure depicting the daughter of Queen Niobe of Thebes attempting to pull out the arrow shot by Apollo. This copy of a classical Greek original from about 440 BC was initially produced for a temple pediment. On the first floor, in addition to sarcophagi and busts of the emperors, Roman copies of famous Greek sculptures predominate: there are two copies of *The Discus Thrower* by Myron (around 450 BC); the *Anzio Apollo* after Praxiteles (late 4th century BC); and *Crouching Aphrodite* after Doidalsas (3rd century BC).
The second floor displays Roman frescoes – including frescoes from the dining room of Livia Drusilla's villa, the wife of Emperor Augustus, depicting a garden landscape complete with fruit and birds. This can only be seen as part of a guided tour. The valuable coin collection of the Italian royal family and a collection of ancient jewelry are also displayed in the Palazzo Massimo.

Palazzo Altemps

In recent years, the important Ludovisi and Mattei collections have been re-housed in the former city palace of Cardinal Markus Sittikus von Hohenem (Altemps), which also reflects the passion for collection and the ideals of the 16th century. Begun in 1477, the palace building was expanded in the 16th century by several Renaissance architects, including Antonio da Sangallo the Elder, Baldassare Peruzzi, and Martino Longhi. Particularly outstanding exhibits in the collection are the *Hermes Ludovisi* (a Hellenistic sculpture of the god Hermes) and the head of *Juno Ludovisi* (a colossal head of the goddess Juno), which was particularly highly prized in the 18th century. A counterpart to the sculpture of the *Dying Gaul* in the Palazzo Nuovo on the Capitoline Hill is the group *Gaul Killing Himself and his Wife*. The *Ludovisi Battle Sarcophagus* is a Roman work from the 3rd century AD depicting the conquering of barbarians by the Romans. But perhaps the best-known piece in the collection is the *Trono Ludovisi* (*The Ludovisi Throne*), which is not really a throne but a block of marble with a hollowed back and a relief showing Aphrodite rising from the sea. It is thought by some experts to be a Greek original, but a modern forgery by others. In addition to the classical treasures in the Palazzo Altemps, there is also a small collection of works from ancient Egypt, most of which were found in and around Rome.

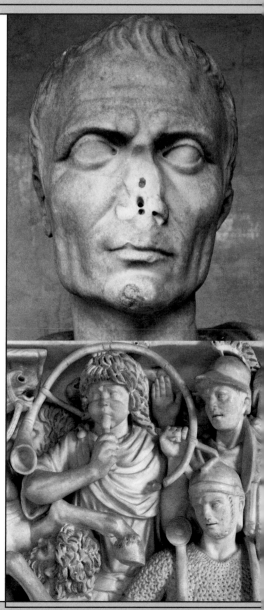

Above: Statesman and military commander, a marble portrait of Gaius Julius Caesar, 1st century BC. Right: A detail of a relief on the marble sarcophagus of Emperor Hostilianus, AD 251.

When the Palazzo Nuovo was built, in 1650, it was styled on the Renaissance Palazzo dei Conservatori on the opposite side of the Piazza del Campidoglio to give the square harmony. A replica of the famous Marcus Aurelius equestrian statue stands in the middle of the piazza, while the original is now in the Palazzo dei Conservatori, where the arm from a statue of Emperor Constantine is also on display (small images, right).

INFO
The Capitoline Museums, Piazza del Campidoglio 1, Museo Montemartini, Viale Ostiense 106; Tel 06 82 05 91 27; Tues–Sun 9.00–20.00; Bus 95, 117, 119, 160, 175, 850.

The Capitoline Wolf

This bronze sculpture of the famous symbol of the city of Rome – the she-wolf suckling Romulus and Remus, now in the Palazzo dei Conservatori – was originally thought to date from the Etruscan period, and the figures of the twins to have been added in the late 15th century, possibly by the Renaissance sculptor Antonio del Pollaiuolo. However, according to new research into casting techniques and radiocarbon dating, the whole sculpture is now thought to be from the 13th century. It has also been

There is speculation about the true age of the *Capitoline Wolf.*

suggested that it was commissioned to replace an ancient statue that had been destroyed. However, other investigations have indicated that the material structure of the bronze is typical of that of ancient times and not the Middle Ages, and consequently debate about the true age of the statue continues.

The Palazzo Nuovo, on the one side of the Piazza del Campidoglio, is the head-quarters of the collection. It was built in 1650, reflecting the Renaissance style of the Palazzo dei Conservatori opposite. The Palazzo dei Conservatori was built between 1564 and 1575 by Guido Guidetti and Giacomo della Porta to plans by Michelangelo, on whose plans the design of the whole square is based.

The history of the collection

In 1471, Pope Sixtus IV donated a group of important ancient bronzes to the city of Rome, which were to form the basis of the museum collection. The statues had previously been held in the former papal residence, the Lateran Palace. They included the

Capitoline Wolf, Spinario (a boy removing a thorn from his foot), the figure known as *Camillus,* as well as the head and two fragments of a colossal statue of the Emperor Constantine. The collection was moved to the Capitoline Hill, and subsequently expanded, and in 1653 it was installed in the Palazzo Nuovo. In 1734, after the purchase of the Albani Collection, the Palazzo Nuovo was converted into a museum and opened to the public – a development that was unusual for the times. In 1749, another collection of paintings was added through a donation made by Pope Benedict XIV. Following the unification of Italy, in 1870

the museum passed into state ownership. It was expanded in 1876, through the inclusion of the Palazzo dei Conservatori and the adjacent Palazzo Caffarelli-

Clementino, along with the remains of other ancient buildings on the Capitoline.

Palazzo Nuovo

The remains of temples dedicated to the Capitoline Triad – the three Roman supreme deities (Jupiter, Juno, and Minerva) – are displayed in the basement of the Palazzo Nuovo, together with part of the Tabularium, the building that contained ancient Rome's state archive, while the ground floor and first floor are devoted to sculptural exhibits. In addition to busts of Roman emperors and philosophers, look out for *The Drunken Old Woman,* a rather grotesque but realistic

Priceless paintings in the Pinacoteca Capitolina include *Fortitudo* by Paolo Veronese (1551) and Peter Paul Rubens' *Romulus and Remus Suckled by the She-Wolf* (1614).

sculpture of an old woman clutching a pitcher of wine, typical of the Hellenistic period, and *The Capitoline Venus,* a Roman copy of a Greek masterpiece by Prax-

THE CAPITOLINE MUSEUMS

The large collections of the Capitoline Museums are mainly housed in three palaces on the Capitoline Hill – the Palazzo Nuovo and the Palazzo dei Conservatori, on the Piazza del Campidoglio, and the adjacent Palazzo Caffarelli-Clementino. Considered the oldest public collection of art and antiquities in the world, the collection was first opened to the public in 1734 by Pope Clement XI when it was housed in the Palazzo Nuovo (see p. 62).

iteles (4th century BC). Two copies of a *Wounded Amazon*, one after Polyclitus, the other after Phidias – the originals were said to have been sculpted in a competition between the two artists to see who could produce the best sculpture – are also highlights of this collection. *The Dying Gaul* is another Roman copy of a figure from the Greek city of Pergamum in modern-day Turkey, celebrating the victory of the Pergamese over the Gauls. It depicts the dying Celt with touching realism.

Palazzo dei Conservatori

The remains of a colossal marble statue of the Emperor Constantine can be seen in the courtyard of the Palazzo dei Conservatori. Exhibits on the first floor include *The Capitoline Wolf* (far left), *Spinario*, *Camillus*, and the remains of a bronze statue of Constantine, as well as *Brutus*, a strikingly realistic bronze bust (look at the eyes) and the pièce de résistance of Etruscan-Roman art of the 2nd century BC. The Sala Marco Aurelio, the new glass-covered hall now contains the bronze (originally gold-plated) equestrian statue of Emperor Marcus Aurelius (emperor AD 161–180). In the Middle Ages, it was thought to be of the Christian Emperor Constantine and therefore escaped being melted down. In 1538, when the Capitoline was redesigned, the statue was moved from its old location in front of the Lateran Palace to the Capitoline Hill and stood in the middle of the

Piazza del Campidoglio until the 1980s. After restoration, and in order to preserve it, the statue in the piazza was replaced by a copy and the original placed in the Sala Marco Aurelio, a new glass-covered hall. The emperor is shown mounted on a horse, one hand outstretched in a commanding but relaxed pose. It became the model for many equestrian statues. The second floor displays collections of coins, ancient stone carvings, and jewelry.

Pinacoteca Capitolina

The Pinacoteca Capitolina is the Capitoline Museums' collection of paintings, also housed on the second floor of the Palazzo dei Conservatori. Dating mainly from the Renaissance period and the Roman and Bolognese baroque, it includes works by Veronese, Tintoretto, the *Baptism of Christ* by a young Titian, *The Fortune Teller* and *John the Baptist* by Caravaggio, *Romulus and Remus Suckled by the She-Wolf* by Rubens, the *Cumaean Sibyl* and the *Persian Sibyl* by Guercino, some important later works by Guido Reni, and *The Rape of the Sabines* by Pietro da Cortona.

Museo Montemartini

Further exhibits from the Capitoline Museum collection are displayed at the Museo Montemartini in a modern, industrial setting in a former electricity power plant in the south of Rome.

The Esquiline Venus – a Hellenistic statue in the Palazzo dei Conservatori.

Rome 175

CITY WALKS

Few visitors can resist the charm of Rome with its bustling maze of alleys and stairways, piazzas and colonnades, markets, shops, and cafés, all bathed in a magical golden light on a warm Roman evening. People come to the city for different reasons – some to experience a little of the capital city's fabled *dolce vita*, others to see the monuments that stand on almost every street corner, some of them thousands of years old. The walks in this suggestion offer the best of both worlds. Immerse yourself in the Roman way of life – there are countless good reasons why "When in Rome, do as the Romans do" represents sound advice – and take a journey back in time into the fascinating history of the Eternal City.

Sights

❶ The Colosseum
Built in AD 72–80, the Colosseum's name is believed to derive from a colossal statue of the emperor Nero that stood nearby. It was once used as an arena for the staging of gladitorial battles and the baiting of animals. It could accommodate 50,000–70,000 spectators, had an awning that could be opened to shelter the spectators from the sun, and a well-planned system of entrances and exits (see p. 70).

❷ The Arch of Constantine
Constantine's triumphal arch was erected by the Roman senate in AD 312–315, following the emperor's victory over his rival Maxentius at the Battle of Milvian Bridge. The arch is one of the best-preserved ancient monuments in Rome (see p. 72).

❸ The Arch of Titus
The oldest remaining triumphal arch in Rome stands at the entrance to the Forum Romanum. It is a memorial to the conquest of Jerusalem in AD 70 by Titus, who later became emperor. The arch has an impressive, balanced, classical shape; the reliefs on the inside of the arch are particularly famous, showing Titus' triumphant return with the loot from the temple at Jerusalem, including the seven-branched candelabra, the menorah.

❹ Roman Forum
The Roman Forum was the public heart of the ancient city and the political focal point of the empire. Temples and state buildings, such as

the Curia – the meeting place of the Roman Senate – were supplemented by triumphal arches, rostrums, halls for legal and business affairs, market stalls, and taverns (see p. 64).

❺ Trajan's Column
The Imperial Forums adjoin the Roman Forum and are today cut through by the Via dei Fori Imperiali constructed under Mussolini. Trajan's Column, erected in AD 110–113 in Trajan's Forum, once had a gold-plated statue of the emperor on top (now replaced by St Peter), and held the ashes of Trajan in an urn in its base. The spiral reliefs narrate his glorious campaigns against the Dacians (see p. 66).

❻ Santa Maria in Aracoeli
In medieval times, this was the political heart of Rome, where the city council met. The Franciscan church, located at the top of a steep flight of steps, is worth a visit for its numerous tombs and a fresco by Pinturicchio (around 1485). At Christmas time, children say prayers before the Santo Bambino, a statue of the infant Jesus.

❼ The Capitol
The religious heart of ancient Rome – the temple of Jupiter Optimus Maximus (the king of the gods) was located here – is today topped by a square designed by Michelangelo. On opposite sides of the square, the Palazzo Nuovo and the Palazzo dei Conservatori are home to the Capitoline Museums. The famous equestrian statue of Emperor Marcus Aurelius in the middle is a copy (see p. 60).

❽ Teatro di Marcello
The oldest surviving Roman theater, on which a Renaissance palace was later built, is today a venue for concerts in the summer (see p. 76).

❾ Forum Boarium
In the cattle market of the ancient city and its adjacent vegetable market (Forum Holitorium) are two well-preserved Roman temples, the rectangular temple of Portunus, god of ports, and a round building known as the Temple of Vesta, which was actually dedicated to Hercules (see p. 78).

❿ Santa Maria in Cosmedin
This church was built in the 8th century on the remains of an ancient temple in the Forum Boarium and one of ancient Rome's food distribution bases. The 12th-century Cosmatesque work (inlaid ornamental mosaics) is particularly fine. In the portico, the Bocca della Verità, the Mouth of Truth, an old drain cover, is supposed to clamp shut on the hand of a liar (see p. 78).

⓫ Santa Sabina
In ancient times the Aventine Hill was densely populated, but today it is a more tranquil spot. The early Christian church of Santa Sabina, dating from the 5th century, is known for its cedarwood door, featuring biblical scenes, and its interior decorated with marble (see p. 126). At the end of the Via di Santa Sabina is the Piazza dei Cavalieri di Malta, with the priory of the Order of the Knights of Malta. If you look through the keyhole in the garden gate, you'll see the famous view of the dome of St Peter's.

Shopping

❶ Gusto Italia di Angelo Biagi
A tempting shop, located not far from the Colosseum, specializing in gourmet products from various small Italian family businesses (wines, pasta, cheese, pastries, etc.). Good prices and outstanding quality.
Via Leonina 76;
Tel 06 47 82 37 00.
www.gustoitalia.it

From left: In ancient times, the Colosseum was known as the Amphitheatrum Flavium; the Arco di Costantino, Rome's largest triumphal arch; Emperor Augustus' Teatro di Marcello.

THE ANCIENT HEART OF THE CITY AND THE AVENTINE HILL

This tour takes you from the high points of ancient Rome via the "Mouth of Truth" to the tranquil Aventine Hill and the famous view through the keyhole.

② Le Gallinelle

Wilma Silvestri knows how to get the best out of different fabrics – some from Asia, some recycled – and transforms them into wonderful, bold clothes, sold at reasonable prices. Visitors to Rome with enough time can commission outfits made to measure. Silvestri's collections are also presented in fashion shows.
Via dei Serpenti 27.
www.legallinelle.it

③ Leone Limentani

In the heart of the former ghetto, this family-run tableware and kitchen equipment company has been trading for seven generations. It stocks classic styles and the very latest designs, and many of the items make great gifts. Make sure you don't get lost in this fascinating shop's many passageways and rooms.
Via del Portico d'Ottavia 47;
Tel 06 68 80 66 86.
www.limentani.com

④ Flea market in the Piazza di Porta Portese

The largest flea market in Rome takes place in this square every Sunday – it's also one of the largest and liveliest in the whole of Europe. Arrive early to avoid the worst of the crush, and keep a sharp eye out for counterfeit products, rip-offs, and pickpockets!
Piazza di Porta Portese and side streets, Sunday from 5.00.

Culinary treats

① Alle Carrette

A rustic pizzeria not far from the Imperial Forums, but the entrance is not easy to find. The oven-fresh pizzas and salads are really wonderful.
Via della Madonna dei Monti 95; Tel 06 679 27 70; Tues–Sun evenings.

② Baires

If you are hankering after a well-prepared steak, head for this impressive Argentinian restaurant. The portions are both rather generous and extremely delicious.
Via Cavour 315;
Tel 06 69 20 21 64;
Mon–Sun 12.00–24.00.
www.baires.it

③ Giggetto al Portico d'Ottavia

Roman Jewish cuisine is simple but tasty, relatively uninfluenced by current trends, and is better here than almost anywhere else in the city. Claudio Ceccarelli buys his ingredients fresh every morning. Try the artichokes and the *baccalà* (dried cod), the house specials.
Via del Portico d'Ottavia 21 al22; Tel 06 686 11 05; Tues–Sun 12.30–15.00, 19.30–23.00.
www.giggetto.it

④ Sora Lella

This trattoria on the Isola Tiberina is a real institution and has been in the same family for more than 65 years. The dishes are typically Roman with lavish portions.
Via di Ponte Quattro Capi 16; Tel 06 686 16 01; Mon–Sat 12.45–14.30, 19.30–22.30.
www.soralella.com

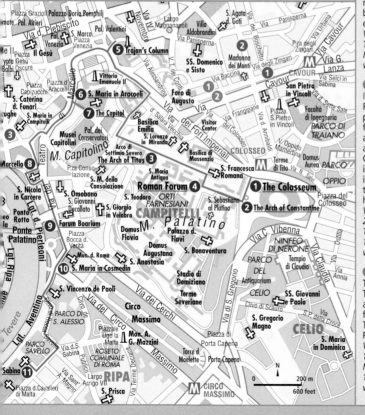

Sights

① Piazza del Popolo
In former times, people arriving from the north would enter the city here. The church of Santa Maria del Popolo near the city gate is a little gem of art history, with works by Caravaggio, Annibale Carracci, Pinturicchio, Raphael, and Bernini (see p. 32).

② The Spanish Steps
Over the Pincio Hill with its beautiful view of Rome, past the Villa Medici and the French Academy and the church of Santa Trinità dei Monti, you'll end up at the most impressive steps in the whole of Rome – the Spanish Steps (1723–26) with their glorious organic curves. The Piazza di Spagna below was once an artists' quarter. Today, it is where the sophisticated shopping streets around the Via Condotti converge (see p. 36).

③ Propaganda Fide
The Palazzo di Propaganda Fide, the missionary headquarters of the Catholic Church, belongs to the Vatican City. The façade on the side facing the square was created by Giovanni Bernini, the façade with the turned pillars on the Via Propaganda by his rival Francesco Borromini.

④ Sant'Andrea delle Fratte
The bizarre shapes of the tower and cupola of this church, rebuilt by Borromini, are striking. Inside, the two angels near the choir are the originals made by Bernini for the Ponte Sant'Angelo and were replaced on the bridge by copies. They hold two instruments of the Passion.

⑤ The Trevi Fountain
One of the greatest attractions for tourists is this fountain by Nicola Salvi. Fed by an ancient water pipe, the fountain is flamboyantly baroque not only in its decoration but also in its use of the playing waters (see p. 48).

⑥ Piazza Colonna
This square is named after the column glorifying Emperor Marcus Aurelius. To its north is the Palazzo Chigi, the official seat of the Italian prime minister, and to its west stands the neoclassical Palazzo Wedekind, with its impressive façade of ancient columns. Reliefs on the Colonna di Marco Aurelio show Roman victories. The crowning statue of St Paul was added in 1589, replacing one of the emperor, which had long since disappeared.

⑦ Sant'Ignazio
This Jesuit church dedicated to St Ignatius of Loyola was built between 1626 and 1680. It has impressive *trompe l'oeil* ceiling paintings by Andrea Pozzo, which increase the spatial perspective, fake a cupola, and blur the boundaries between architecture, sculpture, and painting. A marble circle in the floor shows the best place to stand to enjoy the effect.

⑧ Santa Maria sopra Minerva
This Gothic Dominican church, built in the 13th century over an ancient temple to Minerva, and altered in the 19th century, contains frescoes by Filippino Lippi and Michelangelo's statue *The Redeemer* (c. 1520). The "Elefantino" in front of the church is the famous sculpture of an elephant supporting an obelisk by Gian Lorenzo Bernini.

⑨ Pantheon
Formerly a temple to all gods, this building owes its excellent state of preservation to its conversion into a Christian church. Originally constructed under Augustus, the Pantheon gained its famous circular form (its rotunda) during the reign of Hadrian, topped by a dome symbolizing the heavens, the home of the gods. The classic proportion of 1:1 used for the diameter and interior height of the dome (43.2 m/142 feet) is perfection in architectural terms (see p. 40).

⑩ San Luigi dei Francesi
The French national church is famous for its paintings by Caravaggio – the *Calling of St Matthew, The Inspiration of St Matthew*, and the *Martyrdom of St Matthew* (see p. 44).

⑪ Piazza Navona
In the shape of an elongated oval, built over the outline of an ancient stadium, the Piazza Navona has three fountains, including Bernini's Fountain of the Four Rivers, representing four rivers, the Danube, Nile, Ganges, and Rio de la Plata. Beyond this extend the baroque façades of the church Sant'Agnese in Agone and the Palazzo Pamphili (see p. 46).

⑫ Palazzo Altemps
Past the Renaissance church of Santa Maria della Pace, with its famous baroque façade by Pietro da Cortona and interior frescoes by Raphael, you arrive at the Palazzo Altemps, now home to a branch of the Museo Nazionale Romano.

Shopping

① Borsalino
Makers of top-quality hats for 150 years. A genuine Borsalino is an ideal choice to cut a dash on the streets of Rome for artists and politicians – not to mention gangsters.
Piazza del Popolo 20;
Tel 06 32 65 08 38.
www.borsalino.com

② Elio Ferraro
In the Via Margutta and adjacent streets, you're in the right place for antiques, furniture, and designer items. Elio Ferraro has a shop of 1960s-style furniture, accessories, and vintage designer clothing.
Via Margutta 11;
Mon–Sat 9.30–19.30.
www.elioferraro.com

③ Via Condotti
With the Spanish Steps always in view, the Via Condotti is the ultimate in stylish shopping streets. Chic Roman women and elegant Roman men stroll and linger here while admiring the window displays in the Armani, Gucci, Beltrami, and Ferragamo stores.
9.00–13.00, daily,
15.30–19.30 (16.00–20.00 in summer).

④ Bulgari
Bulgari is the number one address for sophisticated jewelry design in Rome, the equal of Tiffany & Co. in New York and Cartier in Paris. The shop itself is chic and elegant.
Via dei Condotti 10,
Tel. 06 679 38 76.
www.bulgari.com

From left: The Piazza Rotonda in the shadow of the Pantheon; works by street artists in the Piazza Navona; Caffè Greco – Casanova, Goethe, and Liszt were visitors here.

THE NORTHERN INNER CITY

This densely populated area to the east and west of the Via del Corso is the heart of the modern city. Here you'll find picturesque squares and secluded corners, famous churches and palaces, and also lively pedestrian zones, designer shops, and crazy traffic.

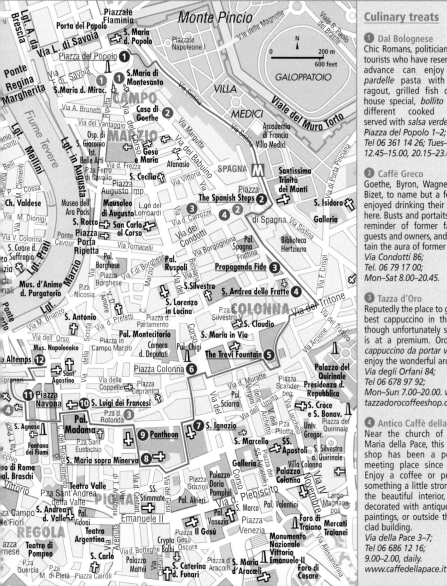

Culinary treats

❶ Dal Bolognese
Chic Romans, politicians, and tourists who have reserved in advance can enjoy *pappardelle* pasta with duck ragout, grilled fish or the house special, *bollito misto*, different cooked meats served with *salsa verde*. *Piazza del Popolo 1–2; Tel 06 361 14 26; Tues–Sun 12.45–15.00, 20.15–23.00.*

❷ Caffè Greco
Goethe, Byron, Wagner, and Bizet, to name but a few, all enjoyed drinking their coffee here. Busts and portaits are a reminder of former famous guests and owners, and maintain the aura of former times. *Via Condotti 86; Tel. 06 79 17 00; Mon–Sat 8.00–20.45.*

❸ Tazza d'Oro
Reputedly the place to get the best cappuccino in the city, though unfortunately seating is at a premium. Order *un cappuccino da portar via* and enjoy the wonderful aroma. *Via degli Orfani 84; Tel 06 678 97 92; Mon–Sun 7.00–20.00. www. tazzadorocoffeeshop.com*

❹ Antico Caffè della Pace
Near the church of Santa Maria della Pace, this coffee shop has been a popular meeting place since 1891. Enjoy a coffee or perhaps something a little stronger in the beautiful interior, richly decorated with antiques and paintings, or outside the ivy-clad building. *Via della Pace 3–7; Tel 06 686 12 16; 9.00–2.00, daily. www.caffedellapace.it*

Sights

❶ Il Gesù
The design of Il Gesù, mother church of the Jesuit Order, built in 1551–84, was revolutionary at the time: the façade and interior influenced many later baroque churches. The decoration of the interior and the ceiling fresco, the *Triumph of the Name of Jesus* by Baciccia, date from the high baroque period, and the marble cladding in the nave is 19th century. In the left transept, the altar over the tomb of St Ignatius, designed by Andrea Pozzo and decorated with lapis lazuli columns, is worthy of particular attention.

❷ Sant'Andrea della Valle
The mother church of the Counter-Reformation Theatine Order, founded by St Cajetan, is stylistically an early baroque structure, built in the first half of the 17th century. The façade has a more upright and dynamic effect than that of Il Gesù, but the interior appears to be less severe. Look out for the frescoes by Giovanni Lanfranco, Domenichino, and Mattia Preti. The Cappella Attavanti on the right of the nave was the setting for Act 1 of Puccini's *Tosca*.

❸ Campo de' Fiori
Every morning, one of the largest and most picturesque markets in Rome takes place here around the memorial to Giordano Bruno, the Dominican monk who left the "correct" path and was burned at the stake here as a heretic in 1600. In the evening the street life in the area is lively (see p. 50).

❹ Palazzo Farnese
The most important high Renaissance palace in Rome, now home to the French Embassy and nicknamed "Dado" (the Cube), has an impressive design by the master architects Antonio da Sangallo the Younger and Michelangelo.

❺ Cancelleria
Another important city palace, built 1489–1513, it was the first to be designed from scratch in the Renaissance style. Built for Cardinal Raffaele Riario, nephew of Pope Sixtus IV, the parliament of the short-lived Roman Republic sat here in 1849.

❻ Chiesa Nuova
The church of Santa Maria in Vallicella has a miraculous painting of the Madonna, framed by paintings by Peter Paul Rubens. The frescoes in the baroque church are the work of Pietro da Cortona. The adjacent Oratorio dei Filippini (oratory of St Philip Neri) is equally spectacular, with its curved designs by Francesco Borromini.

❼ Castel Sant'Angelo and the Ponte Sant'Angelo
The angels on the bridge carry the instruments of the Passion of Christ and were produced by Bernini's pupils, according to his designs. The Castel Sant'Angelo, once the tomb of Roman emperors from Hadrian to Caracalla, then a papal refuge, is today a museum (see p. 106).

❽ St Peter's
Though no longer the largest church in the world St Peter's is still the focal point of Catholic Christianity, and also an outstanding monument of art history. Built to plans by Bramante and Michelangelo from 1506, then lengthened and given a façade and square by Maderno and Bernini, the basilica's interior is home to a wealth of artworks, including masterpieces by Bernini and the *Pietà* by Michelangelo. From the dome, there is a wonderful view over much of the city (see p. 96).

❾ Campo Santo Teutonico
To the south of St Peter's, the German cemetery, which dates back to around the year 800, has numerous tombs of German artists, scientists, and well-known figures.

❿ Santa Maria in Trastevere
The oldest church to the Virgin in Rome, a medieval structure from the 12th century, is famed for its mosaics. The exterior mosaic on the façade shows Mary and saints; in the interior, the mosaic in the apse shows her on a throne next to Jesus (12th C.). Below this are scenes from her life by Pietro Cavallini (1291). The area around Santa Maria, with its narrow alleyways, is a fashionable district.

⑪ San Pietro in Montorio
Within the Franciscan church is Bernini's Cappella Raimondi, and in its courtyard is the famous Tempietto by Bramante. This is considered the most perfect structure of the high Renaissance, its shapes and proportions inspired by the lines of an ancient temple. Legend has it that it was built over the place where St Peter was crucified.

Shopping

❶ Campo de' Fiori
This square has one of the most beautiful markets in the city, with stalls spread out around the statue of the heretic Giordano Bruno. There's a wide range of fresh fruit and vegetables, and the fish is also an attraction for locals and tourists. Unfortunately, its great popularity is also reflected in its prices. *Mon–Sat 8.00–13.30.*

From left: Castel Sant' Angelo and Sant'Angelo bridge; visible from afar – the dome of St Peter's; the Campo de' Fiori – market by day, and fashionable meeting place at night.

IN THE "KNEE" OF THE TIBER, AND ACROSS THE RIVER

This tour takes you through an authentic quarter of Rome to St Peter's and into Trastevere, on the other side of the Tiber, today a trendy meeting spot and bar area.

② Spazio Sette
Situated on three floors of a building behind the façade of a Renaissance palace, this is the best address in Rome for household goods, furniture, and designer items. Beautiful items in beautiful surroundings and perhaps even at beautiful prices, for yourself or as gifts.
Tel 06 686 97 08; Mon 15.30–19.30, Tues–Sat 09.30–13.00, 15.30–19.30, Closed August.

③ Officina Profumo-Farmaceutico di Santa Maria di Novella
Step into this shop and be greeted by a wonderful scent of herbs and flowers. The Roman branch of the well-known Florentine pharmacy (Via della Scala 16, Florence) sells plant-based cosmetics made to the old recipes of the Dominican monks.
Corso del Rinascimento 47; Tel 06 687 96 08; Mon–Sat 9.30–19.30.

④ Almost Corner Bookshop
This shop has a well-arranged selection of English-language books, with a huge assortment of bestsellers and rare titles. If you love books, you can rummage away here to your heart's content.
Via del Moro 45, Tel 06 583 69 42; Mon–Sat 10.00–13.30, 15.30–20.00, Sun 11.00–13.30, 15.30–20.00.

Culinary treats

① Grappolo d'Oro Zampanò
This timeless trattoria close to the Campo de' Fiori offers delicious dishes, including a good selection of antipasti, *salumi* and *formaggi*, as well as different *risotti* and *dolci*.
Piazza della Cancelleria 80–84; Tel 06 689 70 80; in season, 12.00–15.00, 19.30–23.00, daily. www. grappolodorozampano.it

② Il Mozzicone
A simple but pleasant restaurant. After a visit to the Vatican, settle yourself into one of the chairs outside, relax and fortify yourself in style.
Via Borgo Pio 180; Tel 06 686 15 00; Mon–Sat 12.00–15.00, 19.30–23.00.

③ Enoteca Ferrara
One of the most tasteful restaurants in Trastevere, the wine cellar contains over 20,000 bottles, offering a choice of over 1,000 wines. You can also try a glass or two in the wine bar accompanied by a small selection of cheeses.
Via del Moro 1/Piazza Trilussa 41; Tel 06 58 33 39 20; Wine bar: 18.00–2.00, daily; Restaurant: 19.30– 1.00, daily.
www.enotecaferrara.it

④ Vineria Reggio
This simple wine bar is a great place to meet either during the day or the evening; people-watch in the piazza and chat over a glass of wine or an aperitif. The menu is fairly short, but there's a good selection of fine wine by the glass.
Piazza Campo de' Fiori; Mon-Sat 10.00–2.00, 18.00–midnight

Sights

1 San Giovanni in Laterano
The seat of the pope in his role as the bishop of Rome, the oldest and most high-ranking of all Roman Catholic churches, can be traced back to the time of the emperor Constantine. The core of the building dates from early Christian times, but its current main structure is the result of a baroque redesign by Francesco Borromini, and the façade was added in the 18th century. The medieval cloister is worth a visit. Part of the baptistery next to the church also dates back to early Christian times. The adjacent Lateran Palace was the papal residence until 1308; the present building was completed in 1589 (see p. 112).

2 Scala Santa
In a building opposite the Lateran Palace, the holy stairs are said to come from the palace of Pilate and therefore to be the very ones climbed by Christ. They were brought to Rome by St Helena, the mother of Christian Emperor Constantine.

3 San Clemente
The church of San Clemente is built on the site of earlier structures – a Roman palace with a Mithraic temple, and a 4th-century Christian basilica. The Christian basilica is the lower church on this site, with early medieval frescoes. The upper church was built in around 1100 and, in addition to beautiful Cosmatesque work and mosaics, has an important series of frescoes from the early Renaissance,

with scenes from the life of St Catherine and St Ambrose by Masolino and Masaccio.

4 San Pietro in Vincoli
The most famous piece in this church, named after the chains (*vincoli*) in which Peter was restrained, is the monument for Pope Julius II by Michelangelo with its statue of Moses (1513–16).

5 Santa Maria Maggiore
According to legend, this pilgrim church was built in the 5th century on a site where snow fell in August. Much modified over the centuries, the interior is mainly baroque, but the colonnades and the mosaics high on the wall and on the triumphal arch in front of the choir date from the time of its construction (see p. 110).

6 Museo Nazionale Romano
This museum at the Baths of Diocletian houses a collection of ancient statues, mosaics, and paintings; its rooms give an impression of the considerable size of the former imperial baths complex.

7 Santa Maria degli Angeli
One of the most unusual basilicas in Rome; it was designed in about 1560 by Michelangelo, who integrated it into a section of the ancient Baths of Diocletian. Inside the church, the enormous scale of the room betrays its former function.

8 Santa Maria della Vittoria
This small baroque church is home to the Cappella Cornaro (1646) by Gian-

lorenzo Bernini. Bernini captures the intense emotion of St Teresa of Avila, a 16th-century mystic, swooning in ecstasy during a vision in which her heart is pierced by an angel. Members of the Venetian family Cornaro watch, as if in auditorium boxes, from the side walls, in this extraordinary work of art that encompasses the whole chapel.

9 San Carlino alle Quattro Fontane
With its façade of undulating columns (1662) and an almost completely white interior (1634) with complex architectural devices, this church by Francesco Borromini is a high point of Roman baroque architecture.

10 Sant'Andrea al Quirinale
Built by Bernini, 1658–70, this remarkable church building is oval in shape, a solution forced on Bernini by the shape of the site itself. On entering, you are immediately aware of the proximity of the altar to the entrance. The church was once intended for the Jesuit novitiate, but it later became the court church of Italian royalty.

11 Palazzo del Quirinale and the Fontana dei Dioscuri
Originally the summer residence of the popes, then the palace of the Italian kings, this *palazzo* is today the residence of the Italian president. The square in front of the palace contains an Egyptian obelisk and the group of Castor and Pollux from the ancient baths of the emperor Constantine.

Shopping

1 Mercato di Sannio
This bazaar-like street market extends along the Aurelian Walls, and has a covered section. Search here for all kinds of useful items and bric-a-brac, including both new and secondhand clothing, bags, militaria, and rather bizarrely, fishing equipment.
Via Sannio; Mon–Fri 8.00–13.00, Sat 8.00–16.00.

2 La Bottega del Cioccolato
A magical small shop selling handmade chocolates and pralines. Its bestsellers include masks made from chocolate and Roman sights such as the Colosseum and St Peter's, also made of chocolate – tempting edible souvenirs that might not make it back home!
Via Leonina 82; Tel 06 482 14 73. www. labottegadelcioccolato.it

3 Feltrinelli International
A real treasure trove for bookworms, with an enormous selection of Italian and foreign-language books on history, art, food, and travel. There are also art prints and film posters.
Via Vittorio Emanuele Orlando 84–86; Tel 06 482 78 78; Mon–Sat 9.00–20.00, Sun 10.30–3.30, 16.00–20.00.

4 Eventi
Young and provocative fashion for those who prefer the avant-garde rather than simple elegance.
Via dei Serpenti 134; Tel 06 48 49 60.

From left: The interior of the church of Santa Maria Maggiore; the president governs Italy from the Palazzo del Quirinale; card players in a bar popular with AS Roma supporters.

THE EASTERN INNER CITY

Beginning at the oldest papal church, past Michelangelo's famous statue of Moses and the pilgrim church of Santa Maria Maggiore, this walk takes you to some of the high points of Roman baroque architecture and the Palazzo del Quirinale.

Culinary treats

① Cannavota

A traditional Italian restaurant with nostalgic décor. The antipasti is recommended, as are the pasta dishes, particularly the homemade cannelloni, which are fantastic. the food is very good value for money, and the service is attentive.
Piazza San Giovanni in Laterano 20;
Tel 06 77 20 50 07;
Thurs–Tues 12.30–15.00,
19.30–23.00;
Closed Wed and Aug.

② Leonina

A much loved and very busy pizzeria – and no wonder, because these are argueably the best pizzas in Rome, sold in slices, straight from the baking tray.
Via Leonina 84;
Tel 06 482 77 44;
7.30–22.00, daily.

③ Trattoria Monti

A family-run trattoria near the Basilica Santa Maria Maggiore serving some excellent meat, chicken, and rabbit dishes. An excellent wine list as well. Reservations are required.
Via di San Vito 13 a;
Tel 06 446 65 73;
closed Sun and Mon.

④ Ristorante del Giglio

This popular restaurant, located close to the Teatro dell'Opera, is known for its traditional-style cooking and attentive service. It specializes in dishes from Rome and Lazio.
Via Torino 137;
Tel 06 488 16 06;
closed Sun and Mon at midday.

Rome 185

The Piazza di Spagna has been a popular spot for visitors to Rome for some 300 years. It is also an ideal starting point for walking tours of the city. Begin by taking in the view from the Spanish Steps and then head off to explore the sights.

KEY

	Primary route (expressway)
	Major (arterial) road
	Other road
	Side (local) road
	Footpath
	Pedestrian zone
	Railway (railroad)
	Industrial railway (railroad)
	Regional/suburban railway (railroad)
	Underground (subway)
	Underground/subway (under construction/planned)

CITY ATLAS

The maps in the City Atlas section give detailed practical information to help make your stay more enjoyable. Clear symbols indicate the position of buildings and monuments of note, facilities and services, public buildings, the transport network, and built-up areas and green spaces (see the key to the maps below).

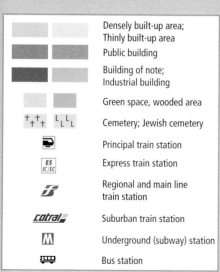

Densely built-up area; Thinly built-up area

Public building

Building of note; Industrial building

Green space, wooded area

Cemetery; Jewish cemetery

Principal train station

Express train station

Regional and main line train station

Suburban train station

Underground (subway) station

Bus station

24 Motorway (freeway) number

ss7 Primary route (expressway) number

37 Motorway (freeway) interchange

One-way street

Airport

Stadium

Exhibition hall

Youth hostel

Car park; Multi-story car park

Embassy

Information

Post office

Hospital

Radio/television tower

Church

Synagogue

Mosque

Column/monument

Tower

Theater

Museum

Library

Viewpoint

Grand Hotel Hotel

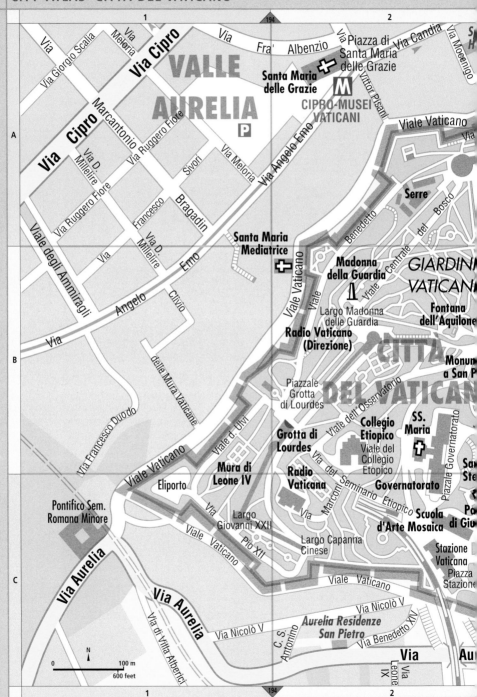

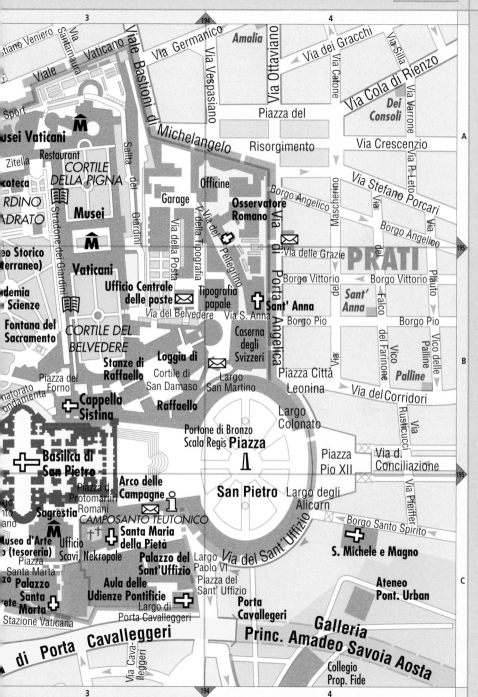

A map of Rome (Vatican City area) with the following labels:

Grid references: 3, 194, 4 (top), A, 195, B, 195, C

Via Sebastiano Veniero · Via Santamaura · Viale · Viale Bastioni di Vaticano · Via Germanico · Via Vespasiano · Amalia · Via Ottaviano · Via dei Gracchi · Via Catone · Via Silla · Via Cola di Rienzo · Via Varrone · Via P. Leto

Sport · Musei Vaticani · Zitella · Restaurant · CORTILE DELLA PIGNA · koteca · RDINO ADRATO · Musei · Salita del Giardini · Via della Posta · Officine · Garage · Via della Tipografia · Via del Pellegrino · Osservatore Romano · Via di Porta Angelica · Piazza del Risorgimento · Dei Consoli · Via Crescenzio · Via Stefano Porcari · Mascherino · Borgo Angelico · Borgo Angelico

eo Storico (terraneo) · Vaticani · Stradone dei Giardini · Via delle Grazie · PRATI · Via

demia Scienze · Ufficio Centrale delle poste · Tipografia papale · Borgo Vittorio · Borgo Vittorio · Plauto

Fontana del Sacramento · CORTILE DEL BELVEDERE · Via del Belvedere · Via S. Anna · Sant' Anna · Sant' Anna · Falco · del

natorato ndamenta · Piazza del Forno · Stanze di Raffaello · Loggia di · Cortile di San Damaso · Caserna degli Svizzeri · Borgo Pio · Borgo Pio · Via del Farinone · Vico · Palline · Vico delle Palline

Cappella Sistina · Raffaello · Largo San Martino · Piazza Città Leonina · Palline · Via del Corridori · Via Rusticucci

Basilica di San Pietro · Portone di Bronzo Scala Regis · Piazza · Largo Colonato · Piazza Pio XII · Via d. Conciliazione · Via Pfeiffer

go ito ano · Sagrestia · Arco delle Campagne · CAMPOSANTO TEUTONICO · San Pietro · Largo degli Alicorn · Borgo Santo Spirito · S. Michele e Magno

Museo d'Arte (tesoreria) · Ufficio Scavi, Nekropole · Santa Maria della Pietà · Piazza d. Protomartiri Romani · Palazzo del Sant'Uffizio · Largo Paolo VI · Via del Sant'Uffizio · Piazza del Sant' Uffizio · Ateneo Pont. Urban

Piazza Santa Marta · zo Palazzo · rete Santa Marta · Aula delle Udienze Pontificie · Largo di Porta Cavalleggeri · Porta Cavalleggeri · C

Stazione Vaticana · di Porta Cavalleggeri · Via Cavalleggeri · Galleria Princ. Amadeo Savoia Aosta · Collegio Prop. Fide

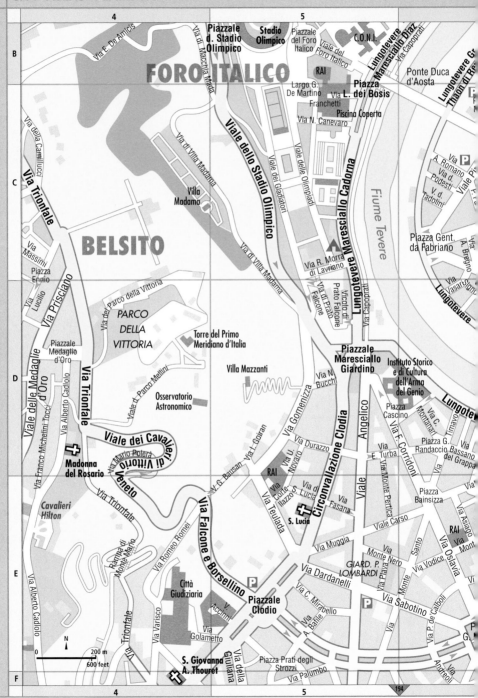

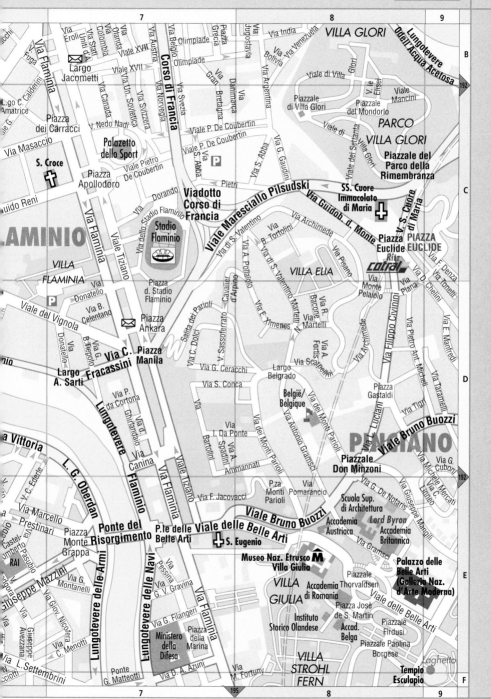

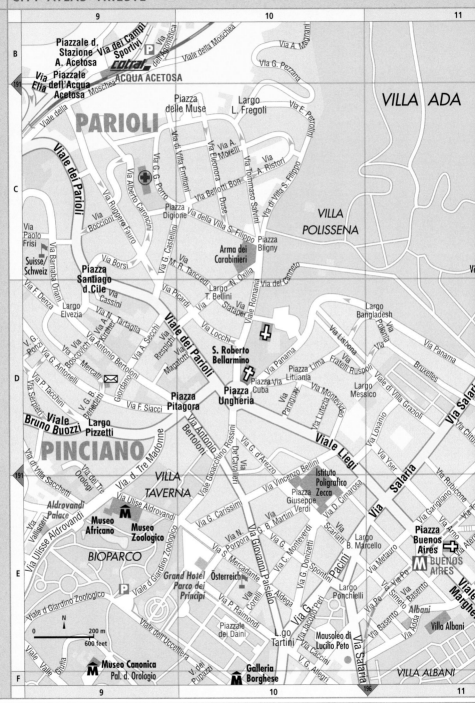

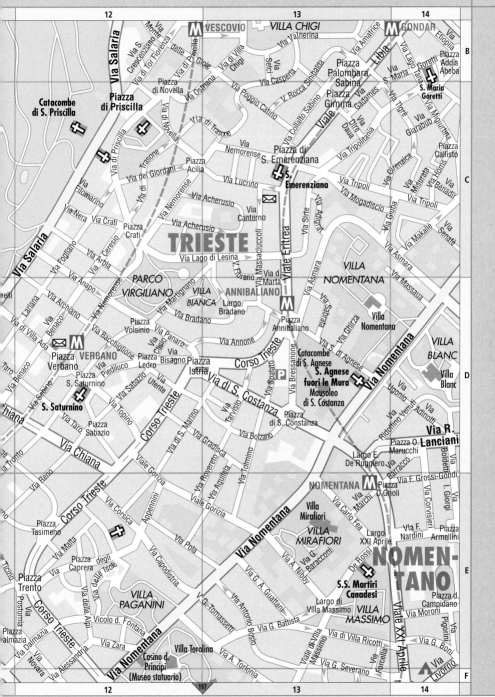

| | 12 | 13 | 14 | |

B

VESCOVIO · VILLA CHIGI · GONDAR

Via Salaria
Via S. Crescenziano
Via Monte della
Via di Tor Fiorenza
Via di Villa Gioie
Via di Villa Chigi
Via Valnerina
Via Selci
Via Casperta
Via Lago Tartaro
Via Goretti
Piazza Addis Abeba
Via Amatrice
Via Etiopia
Libia

Piazza di Novella
Piazza di Novella
Piazza di Priscilla
Piazza di Priscilla
Via di Novella
Via Ostriana
Via di Villa Chigi
V. Rocca Sinibalda
Via Collalto Sabino
Piazza Palombara Sabina
Piazza Gimma
Viale
Via S. Maria Gadames
Via Thirè
Via Giarabub
Via Migiurtinia
S. Maria Goretti

Catacombe di S. Priscilla
Via di Priscilla
Via di Trasone
Via Poggio Catino
Via Dire Daua
Via Tripolitania
Piazza Callisto

C
Via Filomarino
Via Nera
Via Crati
Via di Trasone
Via dei Giordani
Via Trasone
Piazza Acilia
Via Lucrino
Piazza di S. Emerenziana
Via Nemorense
Emerenziana
Via Sirte
Via Tripoli
Via Cirenaica
Via Giuba
Via Misrata
Via Honsi
Via Benadir
Via Tripoli
Via Senate
Piazza Crati
Via Acherusio
Via Acherusio
Via Canterno
Via Mogadiscio
Via Makalle

Via Salaria
Via Ceresio
Via Arbia
Via Foglianо
TRIESTE
Via Lago di Lesina
V. Fioreno
Via di Marta
Via Massaciuccoli
Viale Eritrea
Via Asmara
Via Asmara
Via Sabrata
Via Asmara
Via Massaua

Via Anapo
Via Archiano
Via Nemorense
PARCO VIRGILIANO
Via Martignano
VILLA BIANCA
Largo Bradano
ANNIBALIANO
Piazza Annibaliano
Via Chirza
Via S. di Agnese
VILLA NOMENTANA
Villa Nomentana

D
Via di Villa Ada
Via Bacchiglione
Piazza Volsinio
Via Bradano
Via Panaro
Via Chiop
Piazza Ledro
Via Bisagno
Via Bressanone
Corso Trieste
Via Spalato
Catacombe di S. Agnese
S. Agnese fuori le Mura
Mausoleo di S. Costanza
Via Ugonio
Via Nomentana
VILLA BLANC
Villa Blanc

VERBANO
Piazza Verbano
Piazza S. Saturnino
Via Piediluco
Via Sabazio
Via Utente
Via di S. Costanza
Via Tarvisio
Piazza di S. Constanza
Via Ridolfino Venuti
Via Adinolfi

S. Saturnino
Via Taro
Via Topino
Piazza Sabazio
Via di S. Marino
Via Gradisca
Via Bolzano
Piazza O. Marucchi
Via R. Lanciani

Via Chiana
Via Reno
Via Rovereto
Via Tolmino
Largo F. De Ruggiero
Via Barraccо
Via Boldetti
Via F. Grossi-Gondi
I. Giorgi

E
Piazza Tasimeno
Corso Trieste
Via Corsica
Appennini
Viale Gorizia
Via Nomentana
Villa Mirafiori
Via Carlo Fea
Via Marchi
NOMENTANA
Piazza D. Gnoli
Via Corvisieri

Piazza Matta
Via delle Isole
Via Pola
VILLA MIRAFIORI
Largo XXI Aprile
Via F. Nardini
Piazza Armellini

Piazza degli Caprera
Via Capodistria
Via A. Nibby
Via G. A. Guattani
De Rossi
NOMEN-TANO

Piazza Trento
VILLA PAGANINI
Vicolo d. Fontana
V. G. Tomassetti
Via Antonio Bosio
Via G. Baracconi
S.S. Martiri Canadesi
Largo di Villa Massimo
VILLA MASSIMO
Piazza d. Campidano
Via Moroni
Pigorini

F
Piazza Dalmazia
Piazza Almazia
Corso Trieste
Via Dalmazia
Via Novara
Via Alessandria
Via Zara
Via Nomentana
Casino d. Principi (Museo statuario)
Villa Torlonia
Via A. Torlonia
Viale di Villa Massimo
Via di Villa Ricotti
Via G. Severano
Via Furcella
Viale XXI Aprile
Via G. Boni
Via Livorno

| | 12 | 197 | 13 | 14 | |

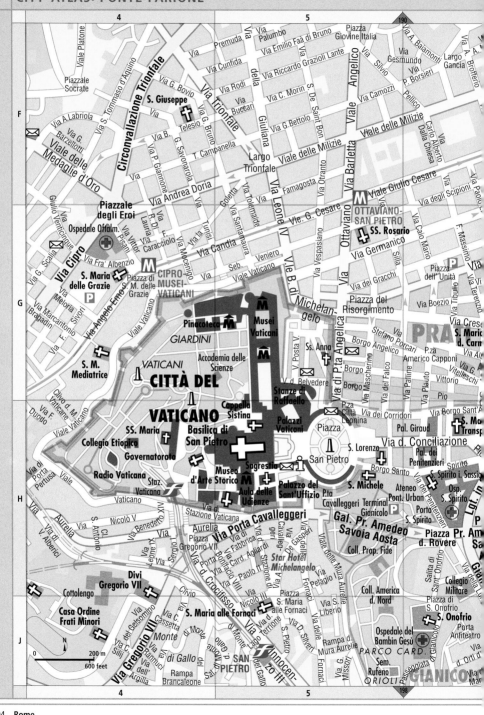

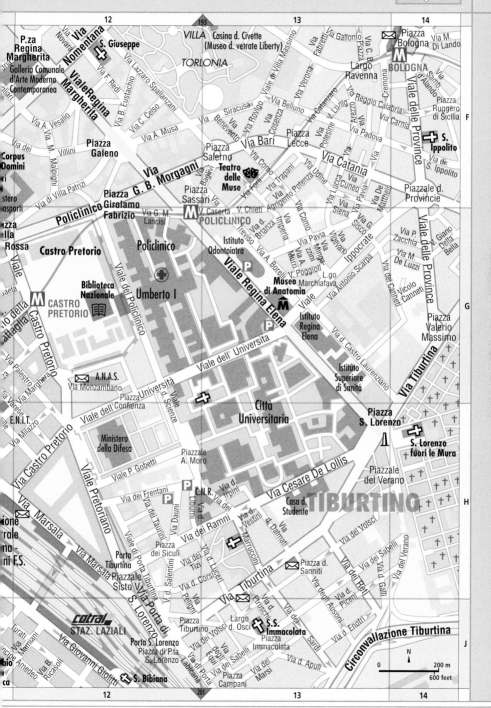

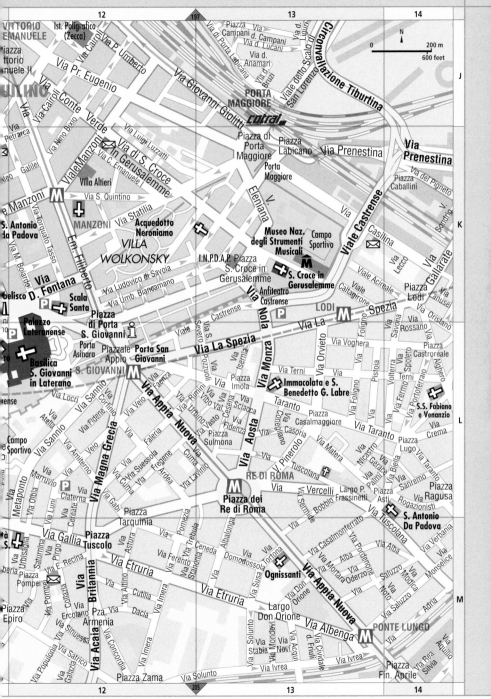

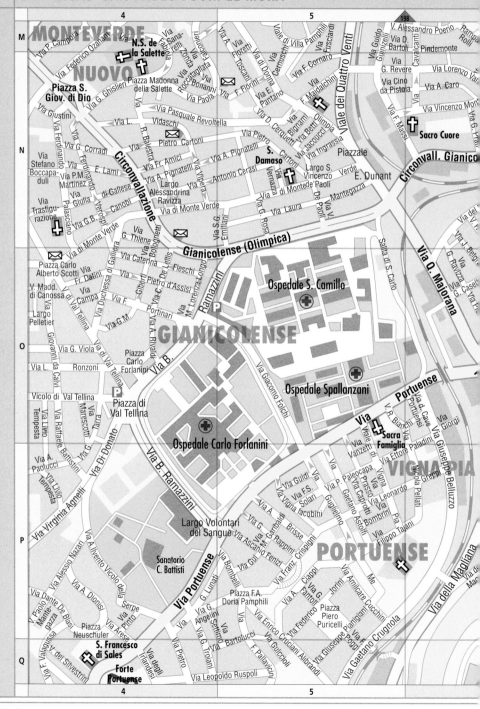

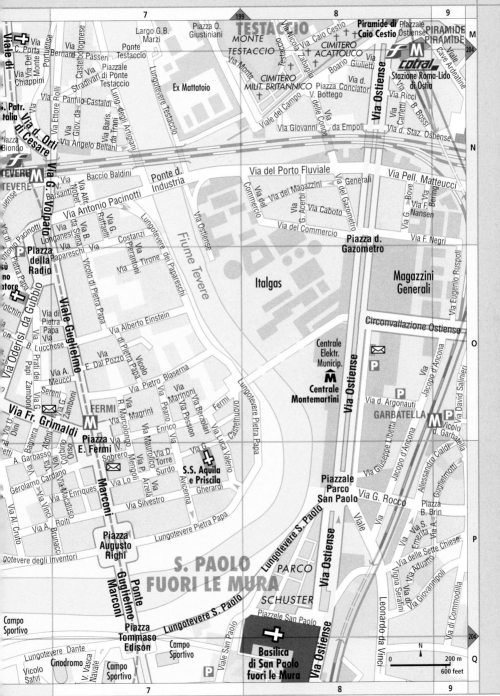

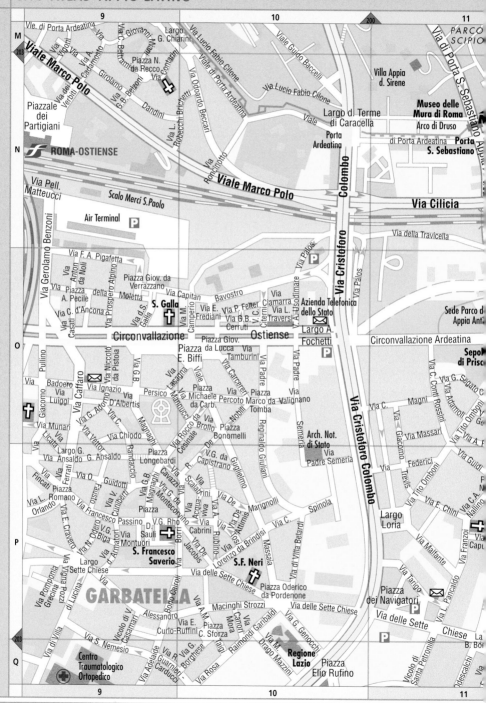

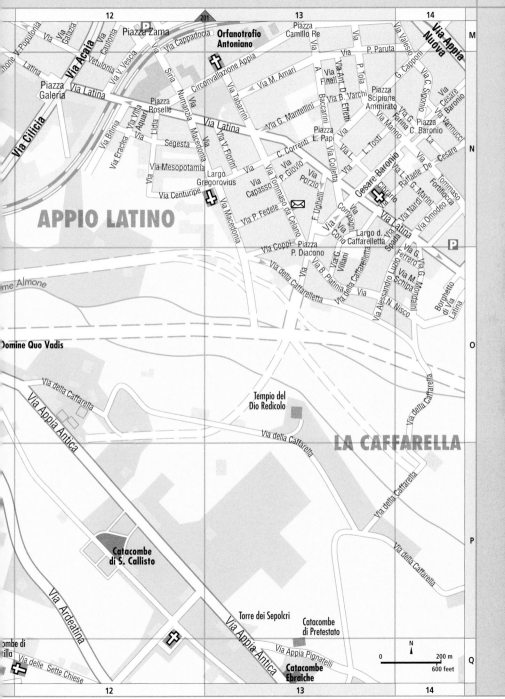

INDEX OF STREETS

INDEX OF KEY PEOPLE AND PLACES, WITH WEBSITES

INDEX OF KEY PEOPLE AND PLACES, WITH WEBSITES

INDEX OF KEY PEOPLE AND PLACES, WITH WEBSITES

KEYWORD	CITY ATLAS PAGE	MAP REF.	PAGE	WEBSITE
S. Prassede	196	J11		www.romecity.it/Santaprassede.htm
S. Sabina			126	www.romecity.it/Santasabina.htm
S. Trinità dei Monti			36	www.romecity.it/Trinitadeimonti.htm
Sacro Cuore	196	H11		www.basilicadelsacrocuore.it
Sagrestia	189	C3		
Salvi, Nicolò			49	
San Alessio	199	L8		www.turitalia.com/cultura/roma/iglesias/chiesa_di_s_alessio.html
San Antonio da Padova	201	K11		
San Apollinare	195	H7		www.romecity.it/Santapollinare.htm
San Atanasio	195	G8		
San Bartolomeo all' Isola	199	K8		www.turitalia.com/cultura/roma/iglesias
San Bernardo	196	G/H10		www.turitalia.com/cultura/roma/iglesias
San Bonaventura	200	K9		www.turitalia.com/cultura/roma/iglesias
San Camillo	196	G10		www.parrocchiasancamillo.it
San Carlo	199	J8		
San Carlo al Corso	195	G8		www.sancarlo.pcn.net
San Carlo alle Quattro Fontane	196	H10		www.romecity.it/Sancarloallequattrofontane.htm
San Claudio	195	H8		
San Clemente	200	K11		www.turitalia.com/cultura/roma/iglesias
San Cuore d. Suffragio	195	G7		
San Cuore di Gesù	196	G11		www.cartantica.it/pages/sacrocuore.asp
San Eusebio	197	J11		www.turitalia.com/cultura/roma/iglesias/chiesa_di_s_eusebio.html
San Francesco a Ripa	199	L7		www.romecity.it/Sanfrancescoaripa.htm
San Gioacchino	195	F6		
San Giorgio in Velabro	199	K9		www.romecity.it/Sangiorgioalvelabro.htm
San Giovanni Decollato	199	K8		www.novara.com/letteratura/depliant/giovanni_decollato.htm
San Giovanni di Fiorentini	195	H6		www.romecity.it/Sangiovannideifiorentini.htm
San Giovanni in Laterano	201	L12	112	
San Giuseppe	197	F12		www.stuardtclarkesrome.com/faleg.html
San Giuseppe	194	F4		www.stuardtclarkesrome.com/faleg.html
San Gregorio Magno	200	L10		www.romecity.it/Sangregoriomagno.htm
San Ignazio	195	H8		www.romecity.it/Santignazio.htm
San Isidoro	196	G9		www.turitalia.com/cultura/rma/iglesias/chiesa_di_s_isidoro.html
San Lorenzo fuori le Mura	197	H14	130	
San Lorenzo in Lucina	195	H8		www.romecity.it/Sanlorenzoinlucina.htm
San Lorenzo in Panisp.	196	J10		www.romaspqr.it/ROMA/CHIESE/Chiese_rnascimentali
San Luigi di Francesi	195	H7		www.romecity.it/Sanluigideifrancesi.htm
San Marcello	195	H8		www.romecity.it/Sanmarcello.htm
San Marco	195	J8/9		www.romecity.it/Sanmarco.htm
San Martino ai Monti	200	J11		www.archeoroma.com/Colle%20Oppio/san_martino_ai_monti.htm
San Michele	189	C4		www.santiebeati.it/dettaglio/21600
San Nicola in Carcere	199	K8		www.italiadiscovery.it/dettaglio_news.php?id=1591
San Pancrazio	198	L5		www.romecity.it/Sanpancrazio.htm
San Paolo	196	H10		www.romecity.it/Sanpaolo.htm
San Paolo fuori le Mura	203	Q8	108	
San Patrizio	196	G10		
San Pietro in Montorio	199	K6		www.romecity.it/Sanpietroinmontorio.htm
San Pietro in Vincoli	200	J10		www.romecity.it/Sanpietroinvincoli.htm
San Pietro, Piazza	189	B/C4		www.romaviva.com/Vaticano/piazza_san_pietro.htm
San Rocco	195	G8		www.santiebeati.it/dettaglio/34150
San Salvatore	195	H7		www.romecity.it/Sansalvatoreinlauro.htm
San Sebastiano al Platino	200	K9		www.romecity.it/ Sansebastianoalpalatino.htm
San Silvestro	195	G/H8		www.santiebeati.it/dettaglio/30600
San Silvestro a. Quirinale	196	H/J10		www.romecity.it/Sansilvestroalquirinale.htm
San Simeone	195	H7		gigiordan.altervista.org/siriagiordania/s_simeone.htm
San Stefano Rotondo	200	L10		www.romecity.it/Santostefanorotondo.htm
San Teodoro	200	K9		
San Vincente di Paoli	195	F6		
San Vincenzo de Paoli	199	K8		www.santiebeati.it/dettaglio/24600
San Vitale	196	H10		www.santiebeati.it/dettaglio/91129
Sant'Agostino	195	H7		www.romecity.it/Santagostino.htm
Sant'Anastasia	200	K9		www.romecity.it/Santanastasia.htm
Sant'Anselmo	199	L8		
Sant'Antonio	195	H7		www.romecity.it/Santantoniodeiportoghesi.htm
Sant'Onofrio	194	J6		www.romecity.it/Santonofrio.htm
Santa Agata d. Goti	196	J9		www.romecity.it/Santagatadeigoti.htm
Santa Agnese fuori le Mura	195	H7		www.romecity.it/Santagnese.htm
Santa Andrea al Quirinale	196	H9		www.romecity.it/Santandrea.htm
Santa Andrea di Fratte	196	G9		www.romecity.it/Santandreadellefratte.htm
Santa Andrea di Valle	195	J7		www.initaly.com/regions/latium/church/sandrea.htm
Santa Bibiana	197	J12		www.romecity.it/Santabibiana.htm
Santa Caterina di Funari	199	J8		www.romecity.it/Santacaterinadeifunari.htm

Picture credits

Abbreviations:
A = Alamy
AKG = AKG-images
B = Bridgeman Art Library
C = Corbis
FMF = Franz Marc Frei
G = Getty Images
L = Laif
UB = Udo Bernhart

Picture credits are given per page, from top left to below right.

Front cover: Alamy/Zute Lightfoot; Back cover: getty | premium | Alastor Photo/jupiterimages

1 L/hemis, 2/3 Bilderberg/Keystone, 4/5 Premium, 6/7 Freyer, 8/9 Freyer, 10.1 AKG/Lessing, 10.2 AKG/Pirozzi, 10.3 AKG, 10/11 top Bilderberg/T. Ernsting, 10/11 bottom AKG, 11.1 AKG, 11.2 AKG/Electa, 12.1 AKG, 12.2 A/Visual Arts Library, 12.3 B/British Museum, 13.1 AKG, 13.2 AKG/Lessing, 13.3 AKG/Lessing, 13.4 C/The Art Archiv, 13.5 C/Archivo Iconografico, 13.6 A/Widmann, 14.1 AKG/Lessing, 14.2 B/Alinari, 14.3 AKG, 14.4 B, 14.5 AKG/CDA/Guillemot, 15.1 B/Index, 15.2 B/Alinari, 15.3 AKG/Lessing, 15.4 AKG/Nimatallah, 16.1 AKG, 16.2 C/A. de Luca, 16.3 AKG/ Lessing, 16.4 AKG/Nimatallah, 16.5 AKG/Connolly, 16.6 AKG/Connolly, 16.7 AKG/Connolly, 16/17 FMF, 17.1 AKG, 17.2 G/National Geographic/Mazzatenta, 18.1 C/Bettmann, 18.2 C/The Art Archiv, 18.3 C/Hulton-Deutsch Collection, 18.4 AKG/Jemolo, 18.5 UB, 19.1 Freyer, 19.2 AKG/ Lafranchis, 20.1 C/A. de Luca, 20.2 AKG/Rabatti – Domingie, 20.3 AKG/Jemolo, 20/21 A/JLImages, 21.1 UB, 21.2 AKG/Lessing, 21.3 AKG/Lessing, 21.4 L/Caccuri, 21.5 L/Caccuri, 22.1 C/A. de Luca, 22.2 AKG, 22.3 AKG, 22.4 B, 22.5 AKG, 22.6 AKG, 23.1 Freyer, 23.2 B/Bonhams, 23.3 C/A. de Luca, 23.4 C/Immaginazione/Osservatore Romano, 24.1 AKG/Lessing, 24.2 AKG, 24.3 AKG, 24.4 AKG, 24.5 L/hemis, 25.1 AKG/ Cameraphoto, 25.2 AKG, 25.3 C/Jose Fuste Raga, 25.4 A/AEP,

25.5 AKG/Electa, 26.1 C/Sygma/Cevallus, 26.2 C/Bettmann, 26.3 G/AFP, 26.4 AKG, 26.5 A/Connett, 26.6 A/Rough Guides, 27.1 G, 27.2 G/AFP, 27.3 C/epa/ Schmidt, 27.4 L/Contrasto/ Lanzilao, 27.5 A/Segre, 27.6 L/Contrasto/Lanzilao, 27.7 L/Contrasto/ Lanzilao, 27.8 L/Contrasto/ Lanzilao, 28/29 A/CuboImages srl, 32.1 A/Wilmar Photography, 32.2 A/Wilmar Photography, 32/33 L/Galli, 34.1 AKG/Lafranchis, 34/35 A/Premium Gpics, 36.1 L/Galli, 36/37 L/Martini, 38 G/Simeone Huber, 38.1 L/Hemis, 38.2 A/Sims, 38.3 A/Sims, 38.6 L/Celentano, 38/39 L/Hemis, 39 L/Hemis, 40 Bilderberg/Ernsting, 40/41 L/Zanettini, 41 Schapowalow/ SIME, 42.1 AKG/Electa, 42/43 AKG/Jemolo, 44.1 AKG/Lessing, 44.2 C/A. de Luca, 44/45 A/Rough Guides, 46.1 L/Zanettini, 46/47 L/Galli, 47 L/hemis, 48.1 A/Werner Otto, 48.2 L/Kristensen, 48.1 L/Galli, 48.2 G/S. Otte, 48.3 L/Zanettini, 48/49 L/hemis, 50.1 L/hemis/E. Suettone, 50.2 L/hemis/S. Frances, 50.3 L/hemis/S. Frances, 51.1 A/cuboImages, 51.2 A/E. Gerald, 51.3 A/K. deWitt, 51.4 A/E. Gerald, 51.5 A/M. Spironetti, 51.6 G/The Image Bank/Krecichwost, 51.7 L/Galli, 51.8 L/The NewYorkTimes/Redux, 51.9 A/M. Juno, 51.10 Look/H. Dressler, 52.1 G/Photographers Choice/U. Sjostedt, 52.2 G/Photographers Choice/S. Huber, 52.3 A/J. Tack, 52/53 ifa, 54 A/Photodisc, 54/55 L/hemis, 56/57 L/hemis/R. Mattes, 60.1 L/hemis/R. Mattes, 60.2 vision Photos, 60/61 L/hemis/R. Mattes, 62.1 AKG/Pirozzi, 62.2 Mauritius/R. Mattes, 62/63 Visum/G. Westrich, 63 C/D. Lees, 64.1 L/Galli, 64/65 L/hemis/R. Mattes, 66.1 C/V. Rastelli, 66/67 L/Celentano, 68 A/Reimar, 68/69 AKG/W. Forman, 69 AKG/W. Forman, 70.1 Bilderberg/Ellerbrock & Schafft, 70/71 FMF, 71.1 FMF, 72/73 L/hemis/R. Mattes, 74 A/E. Gerald, 74/75 L/Galli, 76 A/G. W. Williams, 76/77 A/imagebroker, 78 Bildarchiv Monheim/A. Bednorz, 78/79 FMF, 80 A/The Print Collector, 80/81 A/Lordprice Collection, 81.1 AKG/Sotheby's, 81.2 AKG, 82.1 A/N. Walstow, 82.2 C/A. de Luca, 82/83

Bildagentur Huber, 83 B/Index, 84.1 A/aep, 84.2 A/A. Eastland, 84/85 A/G. Thomas, 86 ifa, 86/87 L/Bialobrzeski, 88/89 G/travelpix Ltd., 92.1 AKG, 92.2 AKG, 92.3 AKG, 92.4 AKG, 92.5 AKG, 92.6 AKG, 92.7 C/Reuters, 92/93 L/Contrasto, 93 L/Contrasto, 94 ifa/Alastor Photo, 94/95 Bildagentur Huber/Simeone, 96.1 A/ArkReligion.com, 96.2 L/Galli, 96.3 L/Galli, 96/97 L/Galli, 98 C/Pizzoli, 98/99 UB, 100.1 A/P. Barritt, 100.2 AKG, 100/101 L/Galli, 102.1 L/Galli, 102.2 A/P. Horree, 102/103 A/Robert Harding Picture Library Ltd., 103 B, 104 AKG, 104/105 AKG, 105 AKG, 106.1 Look/travelstock44, 106/107 G/J. Walker, 107.1 G/D. C. Tomlinson, 107.2 Bildagentur Huber/Bernhart, 108.1 C/dpa/ L. Halbauer, 108/109 C/Alinari Archives, 109 A/AM Corporation, 110 G/The Image Bank/A. Pistolesi, 110/111 R. Freyer, 112 Bildagentur Huber/Bernhart, 112/113 L/Polaris, 113 Schapowalow/SIME, 114/115 FMF, 118 L/hemis/R. Mattes, 118/119 FMF, 120.1 C/Reuters/A. Bianchi, 120.2 C/Reuters/T. Gentile, 120/121 L/Galli, 122.1 FMF, 122.2 L/Gonzalez, 122/123 L/Gonzalez, 123.1 FMF, 123.2 A/E. Gerald, 124 L/Celentano, 124/125 A/J. Tack, 125 A/A. Eastland, 126 R. Freyer, 126/127 A/Bildarchiv Monheim, 127 FMF, 128.1 A/A. Eastland, 128/129 A/Rough Guides, 129 A/N. Robinson, 130.1 A/AEP, 130/131 A/J. Ferro Sims, 132.1 C/M. Listri, 132.2 A/P. Horree, 132/133 L/E. Scorcelletti, 133.1 L/hemis/M. Borgese, 133.2 L/hemis/M. Borgese, 133.3 L/Keystone-France/Faillet, 133.4 C/M. Listri, 134.1 A/CuboImages srl, 134/135 L/Galli, 136.1 A/Photos 12, 136.2 A/Photos 12, 136.3 A/Pictorial Press Ltd, 136.4 C/N. Guerin, 136.5 G, 136/137 A/Pictorial Press Ltd, 137 G, 138/139 G/AFP, 142.1 L/Contrasto, 142/143 L/Zuder, 144.1 G/Photographer's Choice/S. Bergman, 144.2 Bilderberg/F. Blickle, 144.3 G/Bridgeman Art Library/Italian School, 144.4 L/hemis/R. Mattes, 145.1 Bildagentur-online/Lescourret, 145.2 Focus, 146.1 C/A. de Luca, 146.2 C/A. de Luca, 146/147 G/National Geo-

graphic, 147 B, 148.1 Schapowalow/ SIME, 148/ 149 Schapo- walow/ SIME, 149 Bildarchiv Monheim/ F. Monheim, 150/151 A, 152.1 A/CuboImages, 152.2 L/Zanettini, 152.3 A/Spironetti, 152.4 L/Hemis, 152.5 A/Sims, 153.1 Ifa, 153.2 A/Wilmar Photography, 154.1 L/Hemis, 154.2 A/Premium, 154.3 A/Art Kowalsky, 154.4 C/Atlantide, 155.1 L/Hemis, 155.2 L/Hemis, 156.1 Cajho Panorama Images, 156.2 Ifa, 156.3 L/Hemis, 156.4 A/Gerald, 157.1 FMF, 157.2 L/Hemis, 158.1 G/travelpix Ltd., 158.2 L/Galli, 158.3 L/Galli, 158.4 G/Altrendo Images, 159.1 Look/Travelstock44, 159.2 L/Polaris, 160.1 FMF, 160.2 A/E. Gerald, 160.3 A/ Rough Guides, 161.1 C/Listri, 162.1 L/Zuder, 162.2 Bildagentur-online/Lescurret, 162.3 Schapowalow, 162.4 G/MacPherson, 163.1 L/Vanndeville, 164/165 Ifa/ Alastorphoto, 166.1 Bildagentur Huber/Simeone, 166.2 L/Galli, 166.3 AKG, 167.1 L/Galli, 167.2 AKG, 167.3 AKG, 168.1 Bilderberg, 168.2 AKG, 168.3 AKG, 169.1 L/Scorceletti, 169.2 AKG, 169.3 AKG, 170.1 AKG, 170.2 AKG, 170.3 AKG, 171.1 AKG, 171.2 AKG, 171.3 AKG, 171.4 AKG, 172.1 AKG, 172.2 bridgeman, 172.3 AKG, 173.1 AKG, 173.2 AKG, 173.3 AKG, 174.1 AKG, 174.2 AKG, 174.3 AKG, 174.4 AKG, 175.1 vision photos, 175.2 AKG, 176/177 L/Hemis, 178.1 L/hemis/R. Mattes, 178.2 Cahjo Panorama Pictures, 178.3 A/imagebroker, 180.1 L/Galli, 180.2 L/Hemis, 180.3 L/Galli, 182.1 Freyer, 182.2 G/travelpix Ltd., 182.3 L/Galli, 184.1 G/The Image Bank, 184.2 A/Kowalsky, 184.3 L/Vandeville, 186/187 G.

MONACO BOOKS is an imprint of Verlag Wolfgang Kunth

© Verlag Wolfgang Kunth GmbH & Co.KG, Munich, 2009
Concept: Wolfgang Kunth
Editing and design: Verlag Wolfgang Kunth GmbH&Co.KG
English translation: JMS Books LLP (translation Nicola Coates, editor Maggie Ramsay, design cbdesign)

For distribution please contact:

Monaco Books
c/o Verlag Wolfgang Kunth, Königinstr.11
80539 München, Germany
Tel: +49 / 89/45 80 20 23
Fax: +49 / 89/ 45 80 20 21
info@kunth-verlag.de

www.monacobooks.com
www.kunth-verlag.de

ISBN 978-3-89944-485-8

Printed in Germany

All facts have been researched with the greatest possible care to the best of our knowledge and belief. However, the editors and publishers can accept no responsibility for any inaccuracies or incompleteness of the details provided. The publishers are pleased to receive any information or suggestions for improvement.

ROMA**METRO**PER**METRO**

LEGENDA:

- Ferrovia metropolitana
- Ferrovia regionale Roma - Viterbo
- Ferrovia regionale Roma - Pantano
- Ferrovia regionale Roma - Lido
- **M** A Metro linea A
- **M** B Metro linea B
- FS non stop Termini - Fiumicino aeroporto
- Stazione di scambio (metro-ferrovia)
- **P** Parcheggio di scambio
- Capolinea bus extraurbani
- Limite di validità della tariffa urbana Metrebus Roma
- Stazione di prossima apertura
- Collegamento bus da FS Ciampino a Aeroporto Ciampino
- Roma entro il G.R.A. - Grande Raccordo Anulare
- Fiume Tevere - Fiume Aniene
- **FM1** Orte - Fara Sabina - Tiburtina - Fiumicino aeroporto
- **FM2** Roma - Tivoli
- **FM3** Roma - Cesano di Roma
- **FM4** Roma - Frascati/Albano/Velletri
- **FM5** Roma - Cerveteri/Ladispoli - Civitavecchia
- **FM6** Roma - Frosinone
- **FM7** Roma - Campoleone - Nettuno/Latina

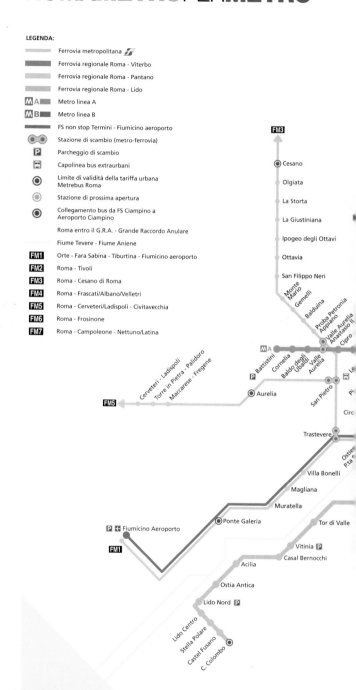